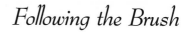

Following the Brush

Following the Brush

FOLLOWING
THE
BRUSH

An American
Encounter
with
Classical

Japanese
Culture

JOHN ELDER

BEACON PRESS
BOSTON

Beacon Press
25 Beacon Street
Boston, Massachusetts 02108-2892

Beacon Press books
are published under the auspices of
the Unitarian Universalist Association of Congregations.

99 98 97 96 95 94 93   8 7 6 5 4 3 2 1

Earlier versions of these essays appeared in the following publications:
"Following the Brush" in *The New England Review,* "Wildness and
Walls" in *Orion,* and "Whalemeat" (originally titled "Whaling and the
Japanese Love of Nature") in *The Discovery Channel.*

Text design by Ruth Kolbert

Library of Congress Cataloging-in-Publication Data

Elder, John, 1947–
    Following the brush : an American encounter with
    classical Japanese culture / John Elder.
        p.   cm.
    ISBN 0-8070-5906-4
    1. Japan—Civilization—1945– I. Title.
    DS822.5.E43 1993
    952.04—dc20   92-13891
                                                       CIP

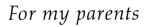

For my parents

Contents

ACKNOWLEDGMENTS   *ix*

INTRODUCTION: *Haiseikaruta*   *1*

FOLLOWING THE BRUSH   *13*

KIYOMIZUSHŌGAKKŌ   *31*

A SHOWER OF STONES   *67*

INHERITING THE INVISIBLE   *97*

WHALEMEAT   *121*

WILDNESS AND WALLS   *139*

CAT'S CRADLE   *155*

Acknowledgments

I wish to thank the following people who have helped me and my family along in our journey toward Japan. My friend and colleague Professor Hiroshi Miyaji has been extremely generous at every stage with his advice, his introductions to people throughout Japan, and his reading of my manuscript. Professor Donald Lopez shared with me the exhilaration of my first trip to that country, while Professors Mutsuko Endo Simon and Nobuo Ogawa were my excellent and demanding teachers of Japanese. I was equally fortunate in my teachers in Kyoto, and I want to express special appreciation to Matsuura-sensei for his instruction in calligraphy and to Okabe-sensei who was my inspiration in Go. Our Japanese sojourn was enriched by friends who took us into their homes and made us feel part of their families. We have grateful memories of the Uzawas and Satos in Tokyo and the Miyachis and Augustines in Kyoto, as well as of Professor Sam Nagara who served as our sponsor and guide from coast to coast. Narasaki-sensei and his faculty at the Kiyomizu School went to considerable trouble to make our children feel included in their new Kyoto classrooms, and we continue to appreciate their efforts. Since returning to America, I have also profited enormously from the encouragement and counsel of Deanne Urmy, my editor at Beacon Press.

Finally, I want to thank the members of my family. Our daughter Rachel and our sons Matthew and Caleb maintained an open-minded and adventurous approach to a way of life remarkably different from anything in their previous experience, while my wife Rita, in Japan as in Vermont, made every day a gift.

INTRODUCTION:
Haiseikaruta

KOMPUKUJI IS A BUDDHIST TEMPLE PLANTED AMONG the steeply rising foothills of northeastern Kyoto. Tourist buses don't often come here, and the temple is not mentioned in the major guides for visitors from abroad. In order to find Kompukuji, you have to get off at Ichijōji Station on the Eizan line, then negotiate a network of quiet residential streets. Behind a wood and plaster wall of the sort surrounding many a suburban villa in Japan's Kansai, the region including Osaka and Kyoto, the modest temple and its modern gravel-and-stone garden seem at first to focus quite a small compound. But Kompukuji's grounds actually extend far up into the encircling woods, and on the slope above is a site making this out-of-the-way temple a shrine for lovers of Japanese poetry.

The haiku master Bashō stayed in a little wooden hut on this spot in the year 1670, when he was traveling throughout the Kyoto region. His dwelling had fallen into disrepair by 1760 when Buson, another of Japan's most famous poets, came looking for it. Though born into a later generation, Buson considered himself Bashō's disciple. He undertook, as an act of respect to his master, to have the decayed structure rebuilt, naming it the Bashō-An, or Bashō Hut. Buson frequently returned to the An to compose with his own students, and to this day admirers of both great haiku poets make pilgrimages here. Bashō's and Buson's poems, as well as those of many subsequent writers, have been carved into rocks and brushed onto wooden placards hanging from trees along the shady paths.

I, too, came to Kompukuji on a pilgrimage, near the start of a 1990 sabbatical in Kyoto with my family. At Middlebury College in Vermont, where I teach, discovering Bashō's poetry had contributed to my growing interest in traditional Japanese culture. I was impressed by the reverberant simplicity of his haiku and by the spectacle of a frail, aging poet undertaking long journeys on foot across Japan's central island of Honshū. During the past decade I had also become more aware of the significance of Zen, and of the Japanese painting and calligraphy influenced by it, for our evolving vision of nature. A burgeoning fascination with the Japanese board game of Go reinforced my interest in such traditional arts—originating like it did in China but rooted for centuries now in Japan. Eventually, after I had completed two years of Japanese at Middlebury and made one brief study tour on my own, an opportunity arose for our family to live in Japan while I studied Bashō and pursued related interests. It proved a richly marginal year.

I do not have, and never will have, the credentials of a Japanologist, so that this was definitely a journey founded upon enthusiasm rather than professional expertise. As a *gaijin,* or "outside person," as well as an amateur, I was constantly aware both of my ignorance and of my conspicuousness as I pursued such venerable Japanese studies as calligraphy and Go. At the same time, it became clear that these pursuits, while traditionally central to Japan's culture, had been swirled off into eddies by the velocity of the economic mainstream. A certain compound irony thus characterized many of my own outsider's explorations: often, I was especially interested in getting to know people who were themselves peripheral in some important sense.

The Bashō-An stood on a little plateau, from which one could see across to the misty blue hills of Arashiyama bounding Kyoto to the west. The rounded, enfolding contours of its thatched roof and the two simple rooms within, one for sleeping and one for composing haiku with a friend, made it seem a snug harbor for a voyaging poet like Bashō. A Japanese friend invited me on an expedition to the An because he knew it was a site that a non-Japanese lover of the poet might never discover. Visits to literary shrines are always equivocal. We may stand in the chained-off rectangle where Thoreau's tiny cabin rose beside Walden Pond or peep into the replica of Bashō's hut, but we always understand that the writers' spirits live most strongly in their books. Still, coming to such places can also stimulate our imagination of vanished lives. In his "Record of Rebuilding Bashō's Grass Hut, in Eastern Kyoto," Buson writes, "At the beginning of the staircase, where we climb up the jade hillside for twenty steps, there is a mound of soil. This is known as the site of Bashō's hut. It is, of course, a quiet and serene place with green mosses, which hide the human footsteps of a hundred years. The dark bamboo forest looks as though in it steam still lingers from his tea kettle." Absence energizes an awareness of *traces*. Similarly, I found throughout our Japanese sojourn that foreignness can become the context for surprising connections.

I picked up two inexpensive souvenirs at Kompukuji. One was a reproduction of the famous Buson portrait of Bashō in his traveling clothes. The author of *Oku no Hosomichi (The Narrow Road to the Interior)* wears the plain black robes of a Buddhist monk, as was traditional for poets of his time. On his head there is a brimless white cap, several inches tall and tilted slightly forward so that it seems a cross between a fez and a beret. A small, square pack hangs in front of Bashō's chest, suspended by a strap around his neck. The poet's face is lined and drawn, his neck scrawny. He is an aging man in frail health, and one who has spent some hard hours on the road.

But the firm set of his mouth shows determination, and his eyes still gaze into the distance. This is the Bashō who wrote, "The days and months, too, are travelers in eternity."

The framed portrait now hangs on my study wall next to a sample of brushwork by the present-day abbot of another Kyoto temple called Tōfukuji. The calligraphy's text reads, "The old pine is talking *satori*." Next to this Zen inscription, Bashō in his robes could himself be taken for a priest. The pack hangs in the right place for a *rakusu*, the symbolic rectangle of patchwork that has been worn around the neck by Buddhists since T'ang Dynasty China. But the master of haiku, although he studied with a Zen master in his youth, was always careful to state that he had *not* attained *satori*, or enlightenment. His eyes never saw through the earth, and his motto remained, "To learn of the pine, go to the pine." Thus it was that he spent the last years of his life almost continually on the road. He was paying a visit to the world, a foreigner coming home.

My second purchase at Kompukuji was a little box labeled *Haiseikaruta*. *Haisei* means "Haiku saints," while *karuta* is an adaptation of the Portuguese word for "cards." This box contains poems by four of the best known haiku poets—Bashō, Buson, Issa, and Kyorai. Actually, there are two separate sets of cards within. The first has the complete texts of famous haiku, while the second combines watercolor paintings with the latter sections of the poems. One player holds the cards with the complete poems and reads them aloud one at a time. Meanwhile, the other contestants are looking at the other, illustrated set of cards, spread face up on the tatami. They try, as each haiku is read, to be the first to touch the card that corresponds to the poem and add it to their own stacks.

The top card on one side when I opened the box was *furuike ya / kawazu tobikomu / mizu no oto*— old pond / frog jumps in / the sound of water. On top of the stack next to it was the corresponding card, showing a long-legged, spotted frog just entering the water, with *kawazu tobikomu / mizu no oto* brushed fluidly around it. Since this is the most famous poem in the Japanese language, even I could have jumped right to the card with a picture of a frog to score a point. But among the fifty haiku were also much more obscure ones. To play the game with success one would simply have to memorize them all and to sort their associated images mentally, according to the seasonal references embedded in every haiku and reflected in the paintings.

Haiseikaruta is a variant of another card game based upon an anthology of poetry almost a thousand years old. *Hyakunin isshu*, meaning "one poem each by one hundred poets," collects *waka* from the Heian era. *Waka* have thirty-one syllables, but only the last fourteen of them are printed on the *shimono-ku*, or players' cards, which are spread out face up. On the other cards appear the whole poems, which only the dealer sees, and which he or she reads aloud while contestants strive to be the first to find the matching ones. Some people credit the development of the seventeen-syllable haiku to the division of *waka* within this ancient game.

My friend and colleague Hiroshi Miyaji told me that *Hyakunin isshu* tournaments are played annually in Japan now. The winners not only have every conceivable aspect of the poems memorized, but they are also skilled at the lightning trick of flipping a *shimono-ku* beyond their opponents' reach. When he was growing up before World War II, however, the game was played mainly by children. All year they worked on the hundred poems, in preparation for the traditional season of games around New Year's. They often didn't really understand the *waka*, since in many cases they are courtly love poetry. Still, they were laying the foundation for further study of literature, appreciating the cards as elegant samples of *shūji*, or calligraphy, and tucking away some lines and images that would become more meaningful as they grew older.

So much of my experience of Japan, as recorded in the essays that follow, has been like a game of *Haiseikaruta* or *Hyakunin isshu*—in which I have tried to spot connections in an exciting but sometimes confusing world. I'm sure that, like the Japanese children of Hiroshi's generation, I have often missed the point, even when managing to tap the right card. But I want to testify, in this era of tension between America and Japan, that out of such enthusiasms at the margin can also come significant and enduring experiences, both of a very different culture and of new possibilities of wholeness for a citizen of today's America. If Bashō's frog jumping into an old pond can represent life's sudden splash within a cosmic field of silence, then perhaps my own flounderings may suggest, much less sublimely, aspects of this surprising moment of intersection between Japanese and American culture.

In reviewing a biography of Lafcadio Hearn, Brad Leithauser wrote that Hearn "symbolizes for us the death of the amateur Japanologist. Gone are the days when a passionate but uninitiated Westerner might cross the Pacific and immediately hold forth on Eastern conceptions of religion, marriage, sex, and art. Such pronouncements now belong, as they should, to specialists—to holders of advanced degrees in Eastern studies and sociology and anthropology, who bring to their disciplines amassings of erudition that Hearn (always happiest when negotiating with the inchoate: with spiritual affinities, intuitions, verses, dreams) could not begin to match."

I love Hearn's writing, as the Japanese themselves do. In his inquisitive outsider's way, he made an appreciative record of their folk-life that the Japanese now find invaluable as they reflect upon their nation's course over the past century and a half. At the same time, I agree with Leithauser that, having learned since Hearn wrote so much more about this incredibly rich and complex culture—through the works of scholars like Benedict, Reischauer, Seidensticker, and Keene—we now know enough to be wary of instant experts. What I hope that the essays collected here may offer, however, is something quite different from introductions, surveys, or generalizations. They are instead personal *stories*, of encounters with Japan's living traditions, by one sympathetic nonexpert. The Zen teacher Suzuki Shunryū wrote, "In the beginner's mind there are many possibilities, in the expert's few." The clarity of expertise sometimes depends, that is, upon quite a narrow focus—seeing sharply by virtue of restricting attention to a tightly limited number of elements. There is great value in such controlled scrutiny, and in the authoritative, well documented reports which it produces. But the meaning of a life and the tone of a relationship also derive from chance encounters, unforgettable conversations, hobbies, and the sometimes funny collisions between public and domestic spheres. Japan is an adventure for me, not a profession. I offer here episodes from that adventure along a cultural edge, where Japanese and Americans stand to discover much more in each other than merely trading partners, competitors, or distant objects of study.

FOLLOWING THE BRUSH

PREPARING THE INK RECALLS A STUDENT TO QUIET
mindfulness for the practice of *shodō*, Japan's way of
the brush. First, the kettle tips, pouring a pool of
water onto the cool, flat surface of the *suzuri*, or ink
stone. This little cast-iron vessel, not more than
three inches in diameter, is surprisingly heavy to lift
when its handle is grasped between the index finger
and thumb of the right hand. It imitates in minia-
ture a type of kettle traditional to the tea ceremony—the upper half embossed with a network of
raised dots, the lid decorated with a slender knob
shaped like the stem and basal leaves of an eggplant.

The end of the *suzuri* that faces away holds a hollowed well for collecting the ink. But most of the
stone's surface is a plateau where the actual grinding
is done. When the stick of ink, or *sumi*, is dipped
into the waiting water and rubbed lightly up and
down the stone, the round pool stretches into a
blackening oval. Some of the ink spills down into the
well. As the remainder on top grows thicker and

thicker, viscous dimples follow the passage of the stick. A sweet, dusty odor rises, like incense at an altar.

When the ink is ready, the liquid in the well is used to charge and shape the brush. Drawing the bristles back and forth across the more densely laden upper surface then firms the brush's point. By the session's end, the stone will be entirely dry once more, but with a shining stain that shows where the ink was originally ground and where the concentrated residue lay longest.

I look at the wooden calligraphy case on my desk. In addition to the iron kettle, the *suzuri*, and the *sumi*, it contains a black square of felt to support the paper while ink is being applied, two long paperweights, and, centered so that it will fit under the barrel-curved lid, the long box that holds my brush. Contemplating this case in which the implements for *shodō* are neatly stowed, I experience the same satisfaction as when inspecting a well loaded backpack or a firmly staked tent. Like those trig emblems of the camping life, the calligraphy box represents release from the world of job and mortgage. My backpack takes me into God's green woods, while the *shodō* chest is the vehicle to an ancient path of eye and spirit. Lifting off the lid on this morning in Vermont, I step back into a practice that began for me the year my family and I lived in Japan.

Like many older natives of Kyoto, my calligraphy

teacher Matsuura-sensei kept the nail long on the little finger of his left hand—in order to signal an affinity with the classical tradition originated by the Chinese literati and perpetuated by the monks and artists of medieval Japan. The long nail, initially an economic status symbol showing that one didn't need to work with one's hands, became over the centuries a token of allegiance to the life of contemplation. It has served as a reminder to oneself and others that there is more to the world than getting and spending; that painting, poetry, and gazing at the moon nourish the spirit; and that beauty, more than either competition or shared wealth, deepens friendship.

Like a *shodō* box, Matsuura-sensei's modest, old-fashioned house was a receptacle for this classical culture of China and Japan. Each week I walked through the commercial heart of Kyoto to reach it, crossing the principal north-south avenues of Kawaramachi and Karasuma before entering a neighborhood of warehouses where trucks and delivery vans rattled down the narrow streets. But when I turned down an alleyway into the center of one such industrial block, I came to the teacher's small wooden house, looking like something from a mountain village. Sliding open the double doors of paper and lattice and entering the studio with its *tatami* mats and low worktables, I could look through the room to a garden. Water dripped from a bamboo pipe into a basin hollowed in a stone. One day a kingfisher alit at the basin as I was kneeling to grind my ink. I enter that world again whenever I spread out the felt backing, smooth the paper on it, and, listening to a robin on the maple outside my study window, pick up the brush.

On the table beside me as I practice *shodō* is my *uri-tehon*, the tall, slender book with a blue fabric cover in which Matsuura-sensei brushed new characters for me to study each week. Within, it holds a single, yard-long piece of paper, folded accordion-fashion. At the top and bottom of each double page, centered on the fold, my teacher painted a *kanji*, or Chinese character. I can open it flat now to display two or four of his *kanji* from anywhere in the sequence of instruction—stark black figures with a commanding roughness that calls attention to fundamental principles of composition.

Lessons were always the same. I would enter the studio, bow, and kneel facing the teacher's bench, then present sheets of paper with my best versions of the six or eight *kanji* I had been practicing since last time. Matsuura-sensei would grind some red ink and brush over my characters, showing how strokes, endings, or overall proportions should be handled differently. It reminded me of time-lapse photography, with his red flowers emerging from my crinkled black buds. Then, removing the lid from his main ink stone, he would charge a different brush with black ink and enter new *kanji* in my *uri-tehon*. I would carry the book over to the students' bench, grind my own ink, imitate the new figures, take my fledgling efforts back up to be overdrawn with red, and go home to work on those same *kanji* for the rest of the week.

This traditional Japanese approach to teaching *shodō* was totally different from all the other educational experiences I have had. Matsuura-sensei never explained any aspect of the practice to me. I learned how to grind the ink, smooth the paper, and wet the brush by watching him the first day. If I wanted to know the proper stroke order for new *kanji*, I had to make sure my mind did not wander as he was entering them in my book. The lessons were not totally devoid of evaluation, though. When he was brushing over one of my own efforts in red, he would occasionally draw a circle beside it to indicate *"yoroshii"*—"that's fine." A solid dot indicated that my *kanji* was getting there. I never received the harshness of an X, with which wrong answers are marked in Japanese schools. He just left an eloquent blank beside the most heavily rebrushed *kanji*. These marks graded my productions in a general way, but they still did not specify what I was to work on. The red version just gave me another chance to study how the *kanji* should really look.

It took me many weeks to see details Matsuura-sensei could easily have told me at the outset. Gradually I perceived that the beginnings of strokes were never meant to be straight across or straight up-and-down. Even though I was supposed to hold the handle of the brush perpendicular to the paper, the bristles themselves were to meet the paper at about a forty-five-degree angle, with the tip oriented toward

Nichi or Hi
"sun"

the upper left corner of the page. In a rectangular *kanji* like *nichi*, or "sun," the upper left corner thus always allowed a little diagonal gap between the horizontal and vertical strokes. Similarly, *kanji* often contained two major horizontal strokes, with the lower one serving as a base for the whole figure. In such cases, it eventually dawned on me, the one on top was supposed to have a slightly concave, upward curve while the lower one should curve down into a balancing convex line.

With some details, even after I recognized how they were to look, it took me long hours to figure out how to achieve the right effect. One common pattern has two diagonal strokes spreading out at the bottom of a *kanji*, into a sort of teepee shape. The one on the left ends with a simple curving taper, but the right stroke proved to be my greatest challenge. It begins thin and broadens gradually, as the bristles are bent farther and farther back. Just before it reaches the bottom of the figure, though, there is a shift. The vector of the brush turns more toward the horizontal and the bristles lift quickly from the paper, so that the ink is drawn off into an elongated triangular point like a claw.

Whatever *kanji* I was working on in a given week, I would devote time each night to practicing this elusive stroke. I could only execute it after finally figuring out a couple of related techniques. At the moment of the lateral shift, it was important to pause for a beat. This motionless moment was like the stillness articulating a piece of music or a dance—an axis around which the *kanji* revolved. The other thing that helped me make this stroke was figuring out just how thick to grind the ink. If it was too thin it would spread out when I paused, making a blob where there should have been a clean taper. But if the brush was too dry or the ink too tacky, the brush wouldn't snap back quickly enough to make a point when the downward pressure on the bristles was relieved.

One night I tried this uniquely difficult stroke with the brush my son Matthew used for calligraphy at the neighborhood elementary school. To my amazement I could do it easily every time, plying that shorter brush with its stiff brown bristles. The limper gray bristles of my own brush had challenged me to gain skills a crisper one would have made unnecessary—and unattainable. My brush's floppy and apparently unresponsive nature came to stand for all of the directions my teacher did *not* give me. Through his nondirective teaching he bestowed a practice centered in looking and doing, not in thinking, and released me from the analytical nexus that so easily turns impulses into calculations.

21

A story I often heard my father tell as I was growing up concerned a certain Chinese gentleman who, because he wanted to become a connoisseur of jade, arranged to have lessons with a famous jade-master. When this man appeared at the appointed place for his first lesson, the master greeted him and, without any further words, placed a piece of jade in his hand and left the room. An hour later the master returned, took the jade, and signaled that the lesson was over. The lessons continued like this for more than a year, with a different piece of jade each time but no explanation. But one week, as his teacher handed him the jade, the would-be connoisseur finally exploded. "I've devoted a great deal of time and money to studying with you and you haven't taught me a thing. You've never spoken a single word of instruction, and this week the jade you've given me to look at isn't even a particularly distinguished piece." I always liked this joke, less for its intended correction of my own impatience than for the "What?" its punch line usually provoked from first-time listeners. But it got me laughing in a new way when I realized that, as a *shodō* student, I *was* that exasperated Chinese amateur—learning, though not recognizing how the process worked. After an American education in the liberal arts, where a high value is placed upon self-expression and originality, I was just beginning to glimpse the value, and the challenge, of imitation.

Kanji-practice provided a serene end to busy days in Kyoto. After settling down by grinding the ink, I would sit at the kitchen table in our three-room apartment, drawing the brush along the paper in the closest approximation I could muster to the new figures in my *uri-tehon.* I felt none of the anxiety of creativity that might have dogged me in a Western painting course. Instead, there was a feeling of excitement and release. Such imitation is far from a passive exercise. On the contrary, while the teachers in the Western tradition whom I have most admired reach out to their students, engaging them on their own levels, the traditional Japanese *shodō* teacher is as immovable as a mountain. The journey out of one's own experience is undertaken, instead, by the student. It is an arduous expedition, this attempt to trace the routes mapped out by earlier explorers.

The settled dignity of teachers in the Japanese tradition insists that learning is the student's responsibility. Yet conformity to a clearly defined norm is also closely related to the pleasures of group identity in Japan. We Americans know about some of the problems related to the power of groups in Japanese society, where work can easily become a rat race and where schools sometimes countenance bullying of students who are perceived as different. But without living in that insular and highly homogeneous country it is difficult for us individualists-on-principle to grasp how deeply gratifying it can be to identify with and participate in one's own cohort.

My favorite image of the *healthy* pleasures of conformity in Japanese schools comes from my daughter's graduation from sixth grade at the Kiyomizu elementary school. At certain points during the ceremony, the whole class of forty would sing a chorus in response to statements by the principal, Narasaki-sensei. The fifth-graders were also in attendance, witnessing the departure of the senior students whom they were now to replace. When the graduates sang their farewell to them, these rising sixth-graders answered with their own chorus of good wishes and congratulations. Back and forth they sang, full-voiced and unanimous, as parents, Japanese and *gaijin* alike, wept at the beauty of this transition between seasons. Then, just before the event concluded, the fifth-graders made a carefully rehearsed, collective speech to their predecessors. One at a time, they shouted out phrases that joined into a single statement. I have never been more affected by a graduation address than I was in listening to the boys and girls of that fifth grade, calling their words back and forth across the auditorium in the gathering syntax of community.

Like many Americans with a strong interest in Japanese culture, my original angle of entry was through Zen. I was entranced by the Zen arts especially, that world of spontaneity and dash, with its runny glazes, gnomic utterances, loony gestures—and splashed ink. As I studied with Matsuura-sensei, though, and tried to imitate the proportion and tapers of his gravely drawn characters, I also began to understand the place of Confucianism in Japan's tradition. This insistence on hierarchy and form stands on either side of the Zen waterfall, and in one sense is also the rock face hidden behind it. Burn the sutras, says the Zen teacher. But the American student needs to understand the implication that one must first *possess* these scriptures before setting them aflame. Behind the magnificent one-stroke calligraphy of the *ensō*, or Zen circle, and the *bokki*, or Zen staff, lie years of training in the way of the brush. Hakuin, the seventeenth-century genius who brought Zen calligraphy to its highest development, first gained the control of eye and hand rooted in *kanji* practice before he launched into the boldness of his paintings.

Respect for the teacher is a venerable Confucianist value, closely associated with the essential Asian value of filial piety. But this respect for authority is in important ways impersonal. Rather than being an innovator, the teacher conveys a tradition and its forms. One Japanese friend, when I described my experience of imitating models supplied by Matsuura-sensei, said that he thought such imitation was fundamentally a form of magic. Confucianism looked back to the mythical sage-kings of China. Because these kings carried out each aspect of their lives ceremonially and with a perfect sense of proportion, the whole land was prosperous. The rains came in season, the earth was bountiful, and the people flourished. My friend explained that Confucianist fidelity to the prescribed forms, both in the arts like calligraphy and in the fulfillment of our duties as family members and citizens, expressed a belief that if we human beings of a later day could pre-

*Sui or Mizu
"water"*

cisely observe the right forms the world itself would become, in that moment, perfect again.

The first *kanji* Matsuura-sensei assigned me were the ones associated with days of the week. At the beginning of struggling to see and execute those deceptively simple forms, I was also entering into a meditation on the evocative pictographs for sun, moon, fire, water, tree, metal, and earth. The *kanji* for water, *mizu*, has at its center a single vertical line, while sideways V's, their points toward that line, burst outward from it. This character manifests the splash when a pebble plunks into a still pond and a star of water leaps out. Subsequent *kanji* echoed this first splash in my mind. For instance, drawing the six-pointed figure of *kome*, or rice—a cross with short strokes radiating from each of the four angles—I discovered a similar starburst of energy, placing these hard white kernels, too, within the sustaining constellation of water.

This sense of entering into communion with fun-

Kō or Ara(i)
"wild, rough"

damental elements of the earth was further en-
hanced by working with *kanji* that combined several
other characters as component "radicals"—increasingly complex molecules arising from the periodic
building blocks. Such *kanji* convey an engaging, elusive poetry, suggesting relationships and pictures
while avoiding the reduction of grammatical propositions. One week Matsuura-sensei assigned me the
kanji for "wild." Pronounced *koh* when standing
alone and *ara(i)* when compounded with other *kanji*,
this character is an elegant construction of three radicals. At the top stands the sign for "grass," a simple
combination of one horizontal line passing through
two short verticals. This little radical is also at the
top of the *kanji* for "flower," and in its smallness
and lack of complexity makes me think of wildflow-
ers—like the delicate white sorrel growing with their
clovery leaves beside our Vermont trails. Below
"grass" is the radical for "perish," itself composed of
two radicals. A single dot atop a horizontal line in-

dicates "hat," while a broad "hook" attached to that line suggests, to a Western imagination, the hook where a deceased person's hat hangs, never to be claimed. At the bottom are the three vertical lines of *kawa*, or river, the left one curving further left as it descends, while the one on the right suddenly swirls off toward the left near the figure's base.

In combination with the *kanji* for "land," *ara* becomes *arechi*, or "wilderness." Entering *ara* stroke by stroke, I envisioned Alaska's Brooks Range where, in the short, intense summer, flowers overflow the grassy banks of rivers rushing with snowmelt and where, in any season, it would take only one careless slip for a hiker to perish. This romantic image of bones in the wilderness revolved toward a more integrated view as I painted, though, helped by the fact that "perish" is held up and balanced between the river and the blossoming meadows, part of the fabric rather than an extraneous side effect or dramatic contrast. Death in that landscape is not an accident. It is one with the rough surges of life that shove the wilderness into flower, propelling life on its journey across the snow. The poetry of wild landscapes flows into the dictionary's long column of compounds which are formed by combining *ara* with various other *kanji*. Among these are the characters for rough seas, high mountains, courage, sexual indulgence, ruin, robbery, and eagles—painting a world of attractive danger, ironic connections.

Walking across town to Matsuura-sensei's house, I made my way first through the throngs of Gion, Kyoto's entertainment district, then passed the busi-

Moku or Ki
"tree"

ness district, its air filled with the din of construction and the fumes of bus exhaust. Turning down the alleyway where the teacher waited serenely behind his sliding door always felt like stepping back into a sustaining memory. Evenings, in our family's crowded apartment in the Higashiyama district, I felt a similar energy as I smoothed out a blank new page and prepared my ink. Wordsworth writes in "Tintern Abbey" of "an eye made quiet by the power / Of harmony." Looking closely at the beautiful brings its blessing.

Following the brush of an ancient Asian tradition, a modern Westerner may be nourished by the example of generations who devoted themselves to imitating, and perpetuating, a world of beautiful forms. The *kanji* for *ki,* or "tree," expresses nature as well as culture in its four strokes. A vertical line expresses the tree's thrust toward the sun, while outward diagonals, diverging halfway down this line and fanning out to define, with it, a three-pointed base, suggest the graceful sweep of an evergreen. But across the top, where those lines start, is a horizontal line distinguishing the outline from what might otherwise appear a child's version of a Christmas tree. I remembered this exposed line when hiking on Mt. Abraham near my house last week. It is one of the few mountains in Vermont that rises above tree line. As the spruces near the summit shrank in height before giving way to the granite ridge, I could observe how often they were bare of needles near the crown—trees rising above their own tree line. Dead branches, showing the effects of acid rain, continued to reach out for the sun and to arrest passing hikers for a moment's comprehension.

Paying attention to the trees may be the most important challenge for us in the industrialized world now, as a way both to understand the magnitude of danger posed by our destructive behavior and to escape from the noisy distractions of our egotistical, self-assertive agendas. Bashō writes, "Yield to the willow / All the loathing, all the desire / Of your heart" (*Haiku*, trans. R. H. Blyth, Tokyo: Hokuseido, 1949). We need now to identify and practice disciplines that will bring us back to earth, offering the relief of yielding to a larger world. This is the testimony of the brush, modestly following, stroke by stroke, the outlines of a world that blossoms from the ink.

KIYOMIZU-
SHŌGAKKŌ

*

Kiyomizu, "Pure Water."
Shōgakkō, "Elementary School."

Narasaki-sensei, principal of Kiyomizushō-gakkō, interviewed us in an office crowded with furniture and memorabilia. Two large sofas faced each other across a low table, with a pair of upholstered chairs defining each of the rectangle's other two sides. The principal's massive desk stood in front of a draped window, while filing cabinets, bookshelves, and display cabinets covered the lower walls. In a continuous row above these furnishings were photographs of the school's previous principals. A number of men in the earliest of these pictures wore the robes of Buddhist priests. As the series of images entered the twentieth century, Edwardian collars rose, then subsided, while eyeglasses became steadily more common. The last half-dozen principals were uniformly dressed in the black suit, white shirt, and dark tie of the modern *sarariman* ("salaryman"). Behind the cabinets' glass doors we could see ribbons, pennants, and silver trophies commemorating the achievements of orchestras and baseball

33

teams that had represented this venerable school over the decades. But more striking than all these prizes was an enormous stuffed sea turtle, varnished and gleaming atop a table near the door. We realized later, having also noted stylized turtles on the school's flag and on manhole covers all over town, that this was an ancient symbol of Kyoto.

The atmosphere of this office was far from either the simplicity of a Japanese tea cottage or the chrome and glass elegance of today's Tokyo. Rather, it evoked the fascinating smother of a Victorian drawing room, reflecting the fact that Kiyomizushōgakkō had been founded at the end of the last century. It was one of a wave of Western-style schools inspired by Commodore Perry's appearance in the mid-nineteenth century and the subsequent Meiji Restoration. After the social stagnation of their final century under the Tokugawa shoguns, the Japanese were eager to adopt modern ways. They imported consultants from Europe and America to help institute reforms in such areas as education, medicine, postal service, and transportation.

Kiyomizushōgakkō is architecturally reminiscent of public schools founded in American cities during the same period, with their high ceilings and oak banisters. A formal stone stairway ascends from street level to the wide doorway of the main building, whose external walls are tan stucco under a tile roof. Spacious halls connect the classrooms, music rooms, and gymnasium into a U. The high windows are undraped in all of the rooms except the principal's formal office, and I never saw an electric light burning during my many other daytime visits to the school. Nor is there any central heating so far as I could tell. Students simply wear heavy sweaters during the cold weeks of January and February. And, to my surprise, they keep their shoes on, even in the classrooms. The courtyard enclosed by the school's wings contains a large, wire-mesh aviary housing a variety of fowl both domestic and ornamental. Beside it is a pond where fat carp, orange, white, black, and every combination of the three colors, circle slowly, occasionally rising to mouth the surface.

But before touring the school, much less enrolling our children in it, my wife Rita and I had to work to convince Narasaki-sensei that we belonged there. Until right before we left Vermont, we had been expecting to live in a different district of Kyoto. We had made preliminary contact with the principal of that neighborhood's school—in the north-central part of the city, near Kyoto and Dōshisha Universities. There were frequently foreign families living in that district with their children, and the schools knew how to deal with them. Kiyomizushōgakkō, on the other hand, lies in the city's eastern foothills near the famous Kiyomizu Temple, and is largely a neighborhood of artisans and shopkeepers. In its century of existence the school had never had a single *gaijin* among its pupils.

Narasaki-sensei's hesitation about allowing our children into his school was not simply from inexperience with the pertinent regulations and funding arrangements. He reasonably pointed out that neither he nor the teachers who would have Rachel, Matthew, and Caleb in class spoke English, while for their part the children knew barely any Japanese. This would severely hamper their ability to follow along in literature, history, or social studies, and he wondered if, rather than having them fall behind in such subjects, it might not be better to place them in an international school. We responded that they would still be able, with our help, to do math, science, and art, and that by doing their best to pay attention in other subjects they would get the chance to pick up some more Japanese. Besides, we viewed this chance to experience another school system, and culture, from within as a rare opportunity for them. It would do much to enrich their outlook on the world when they returned to the homogeneous, rural schools of Bristol, Vermont. Over an afternoon of bitter green tea and little confections made of bean paste, we circled around and around these issues like carp measuring the circumference of a pond.

Although Rita was to learn a good bit of Japanese during our Kyoto sojourn, her studies had not begun when we met with Narasaki-sensei. She had just come along with me as a gesture of solidarity. Nor had my study of the language at Middlebury College prepared me for this torrent of highly formal Japanese with a strong Kyoto accent. I clung to those words that I did understand, my mind racing to infer what the main point of each sentence was. Both my chief resource and my pitfall in this conversation was the phrase *Sō desu ka*, "Is that so?" It's considered polite in Japanese to murmur such phrases frequently, in order to let the person who is speaking know that you're following with interest. The phrase *Sō desu ne,* or "No kidding!" was one I threw in for variety from time to time, as Narasaki-sensei told us about the school and about the procedures for registering as alien residents with the prefectural office. The advantage of these phrases was that they bought me time, by encouraging Narasaki-sensei to believe that communication was taking place. And indeed, when I listened for five minutes at a stretch I could usually get his gist. But my formulaic niceties were also deceptive, in suggesting that I understood the content of what he was saying sentence by sentence. So that on those occasions when he suddenly stopped for an answer or a lengthier comment from me, I would have to engage in frantic guesswork before coming up with some little set speech about the nature of my research project or of my children's schooling in Vermont.

It's greatly to the credit of Narasaki-sensei, and to that of Fuji-san, the school's secretary who sat with us presiding over the refreshments, that neither burst out laughing during this event. I'm sure that my speeches must often have resembled those made by my grandmother at our dinner table as I was growing up. Though largely deaf, she refused to wear a hearing aid. Still, being an irrepressibly sociable being, she would from time to time burst animatedly and randomly into whatever discussion was going on. I remember as a teenager being delighted and amazed by the way she could turn our family's conversation on a dime. A consideration of the Giants' chances in the pennant race instantly modulated into a lament for the declining quality of seafood or a rehashing of the latest episode of *As the World Turns*. Sometimes, as such examples suggest, there was a startling inner logic to these random copulars. I can only hope that Rita and I were as diverting for Narasaki-sensei as my grandmother's sudden veers always remained to me.

I don't know whether it was in response to something I had just said, but after a couple of hours of our circling companionably toward understanding in Narasaki-sensei's office, he suddenly stood up and announced that he was ready to come to our apartment with us. My two provisional theories at the time were: (1) that it was an inspection, to ascertain that we were actually in the school district and that we lived in a decent manner, or (2) that he had just decided to let our children enroll and was immediately reciprocating our visit to him with a courtesy call. Rita and I panicked at this turn of events, since there were clothes hanging out to dry on our balcony and we had left the children lounging around in their pajamas, recovering from jet lag by watching exotic cartoons and game shows on television. We arranged in whispers on our walk to the apartment building that I would usher Narasaki-sensei into the public parlor while Rita hustled down the hall to roust the kids into shape and put on a kettle for tea. In fact he ended up staying only about ten minutes in all before strolling back to the school, assuring us with a smile and a wave that our kids could start attending their classes the next day.

Our children's initial experience at Kiyomizushō-gakkō mirrored our interview with Narasaki-sensei in certain ways. They felt baffled and embarrassed, and undoubtedly provoked similar feelings both in their new teachers and in their fellow students. Who were these new fish in the pond? The mutual shock resulted in part from racial difference. The population of Vermont is by all measures the least diverse of any state in the Union. Even so, the homogeneity of Bristol could not compare with what our three kids found on the Kiyomizushōgakkō playground. The reality that they were the first foreigners to set foot there was reinforced by the fact that every other child, without exception, had black hair and brown eyes. Since our Rachel is a blonde with brown eyes, while Matthew has brown hair, Caleb has red hair, and both boys have blue eyes, their schoolmates wanted to know both where they came from and if they really went together. Their appearance provoked amazed laughter wherever they turned, while the sixth-grade boys alternated showing them the peace sign and giving them the finger, in a process of cultural diffusion traveling along the backwash of *Easy Rider.* Caleb the Red was singled out for special attention and ended his first week of school by being pushed into the pond by someone he'd never even seen come up behind him.

But one advantage of this occasionally brutal process of immersion was that all three of our children soon learned to swim. Caleb, an absentminded nine-year-old with a strong sense of fantasy, had never really found a best friend before going to Japan. In his new classmate named Keishi, though, he did discover such a soulmate. They were exactly the same height and within a day of the same age, so that they celebrated their birthdays together in April during our stay. They also found that they could communicate successfully through play even before they had much language in common, and that their racial difference was both nonessential and an amusing detail. Keishi liked to tousle Caleb's red mop and say, "Spa-ga-ga-ghetti!" and Caleb responded by flipping Keishi's head of equally thick black hair with his fingertips while chanting "Yaki Soba," the name of the dark buckwheat noodles we sometimes ate at a neighborhood restaurant. Or Caleb would refer to his new friend as *keshi-gomu,* or "rubber eraser," one of the words he had just picked up in class. First came the intuition of connection, and then, piece by piece, they put together the silly rituals and nicknames that gave friendship a voice.

In class, too, our children proceeded from guesswork and intuition. In a funny way, inference worked better for them in a Japanese school than it might have elsewhere, precisely because the subjects were presented in the *opposite* of such an inductive approach. Rote is not a dirty word in Japan. In part this relates to the Confucian model of imitation I was experiencing in my own encounters with the traditional study of calligraphy. But it also reflects the nature of the Japanese language. The grammar is highly complex, and in addition there are three written systems to learn. A child's first alphabet is the *hiragana*, forty-six symbols which, along with certain diacritical marks that can turn an h-sound into either a b- or a p-, can describe all of the sounds in Japanese. Young pupils must also soon learn the *katakana*, a similar syllabary used for foreign words and for special purposes such as telegrams. Since a great many foreign words have been absorbed into Japanese, especially in the worlds of advertising, fashion, and technology, *katakana* get used a lot. But although those two systems already demand much more of Japanese students than our alphabet does of ours, they are only a preliminary to the real challenge—learning *kanji*.

By the time they are in sixth grade, Japanese students are expected to know and use a list of 881 *kanji*, and by the time they complete high school they should have mastered about 1900. A given character can often include over twenty strokes. Though the most complex ones are frequently built up of the basic components called radicals, the fact that each radical may be used within a number of different *kanji* is a source of confusion as much as it is an aid to memory. I've never had the opportunity to study Chinese, but I have the impression that learning to write is more challenging for the Japanese than for other nations employing the *kanji*. For one thing, even though Chinese students have to memorize many more of these characters, that is the *only* written system they have to learn. Not only do

Japanese constantly have to add *hiragana* in writing, to indicate verb endings, prefixes, suffixes, and other elements unnecessary in Chinese, but they also give various readings to particular *kanji*. In China the sounds of characters have changed over time, but a given symbol has only had one reading in each period and region. By contrast, in Japan these symbols came across in several waves, separated by centuries, and from parts of China where they were pronounced entirely differently. Thus, when the Japanese combined characters to spell out their own words they used them to indicate a variety of sounds in the different compounds. To take a basic example, the counter "one" is indicated by a single horizontal line in Chinese and Japanese, but in certain contexts Japanese schoolchildren must learn to vocalize that symbol as *ichi, hi, hito(tsu)*, and *itsu*. For all of these reasons, Japanese, like foreigners, find it hard to learn their own language, and spend much more time on the rudiments of writing than students in America do on English. The complexity of written Japanese is such a burden that there have twice been long and serious debates in the Japanese Diet about changing the national language. Early in the twentieth century, the proposal was to adopt French instead, allowing Japanese to die out with the elderly generation, whereas English was the suggested replacement after World War II.

In addition to the central place of *kanji* memorization in Japanese schooling, there is a strong emphasis on rote in the teaching of mathematics. Our

Caleb has always been disappointed not to have more challenging math in his American schools. Thus, we all looked forward to that aspect of Japanese schooling for him. The Japanese are at least a year ahead of our students in the level of math studied in a given year. In the *mastery* of what they study, as measured by standardized tests, their students lead the world. By contrast, Americans test far behind every industrialized nation in Asia and every single country in western Europe. We discovered that the central activity in our children's Japanese math classes was speed calculation. Caleb had to hold onto his hat when, in his third-grade class, the children added and multiplied three-digit columns of numbers. It's hard for me to imagine that any children could better those Japanese students' results for both speed and accuracy.

The initial contrast with our Vermont schools that struck Rita and me most strongly was the extremely high standard of competence shown by Japanese students in basic skills of reading and computation. Our impression, in these regards, was that almost all of their students performed at a much better level than all but the best of ours. On the other hand, there were two aspects of the elementary curriculum in our little rural Vermont school that we far preferred. One was our own schools' emphasis on constant *writing*, as the context both for developing language skills and for thinking about diverse subjects. My impression was that essay writing was not as central a part of the education at Kiyomizushōgakkō. For all the limitations of our American schools, encouraging students both to express themselves and to formulate and defend an argument remains a great service they provide to us as a democracy.

Similarly, the mathematics program called Math Their Way which is often used in Vermont gets students to think about the concepts and patterns *behind* their calculations, right from the beginning. I once had a conversation with a professor of mathematics at the Tōhoku University in Sendai. Professor Oda told me that, even though Japanese high school graduates have the highest mathematical skills of anyone their age in the world, the culmination of their work is the entrance examination for university. Few pursue higher mathematics thereafter or become capable of carrying out graduate study in that subject. Those who do go on for Ph.D.'s often choose to study in the United States, where, at the top level, mathematical education is incomparably stronger.

These first impressions on the ground in Kyoto thus confirmed the assumptions we arrived with about Japanese efficiency versus American independence. But such a stark contrast broke down for us as we were exposed longer to the educational approach at Kiyomizushōgakkō. Americans often associate rote learning with grinding, soulless labor, from which the school bell releases children with a clang that is followed closely by a wild, collective whoop. We console ourselves for our incompetence by picturing the Japanese at all ages as drudges. But what our family saw at the elementary level suggested that the mental and emotional pressure of school in Kyoto was actually less than in Bristol. For one thing, there is an enjoyably *physical* aspect to much of the memorization. Each of our children came back from Japan with a calligraphy set and a *soroban*, or Japanese abacus, that are still among their most prized possessions. These were the implements that made practicing their writing and calculation fun.

To learn *kanji* in a Japanese school is also to learn classical calligraphy with a brush. Our children and I often sat down together at the kitchen table after supper. We covered the surface with newspaper, ground our own supplies of ink with our ink sticks, and began to paint the characters we had been assigned by our respective teachers. Though my instruction was through private lessons with an old man across town who dressed in monk's robes and theirs was in a classroom with forty children and a teacher dressed in casual modern clothing, we shared the same excitement about working with these supple brushes and profoundly black ink. And sometimes we would be applying ourselves to the same *kanji*. I remember one session where Matthew and I were both practicing *gatsu* or *tsuki*, the character for "moon." It's one of the most common *kanji* in compounds, and one of the most elusive and elegant. The first stroke is a vertical that sweeps slightly to the left as it approaches the bottom reach. Then comes a slightly rising horizontal that reaches a corner, turns it with a strong elbow, and rushes downward in rough parallel with the first stroke. At the

Gatsu or Tsuki
"moon"

bottom the brush is simultaneously lifted and swept up toward the upper left corner, creating a stroke that frays into the whiteness of the paper. Inside the vertical rectangle that has now been outlined go two horizontal strokes. Four strokes in all, then, perhaps representing a crescent moon barred with a wisp of cloud. But in its proportions, its turnings, and the variation of its stroke-endings, endlessly challenging.

This is not the rote of flashcards, but a process of repetition more akin to a sacramental ritual. Especially in a culture where calligraphy ranks so high among the traditional arts, a young student's first efforts at painting the *kanji* have a definite glamor and status in everyone's eyes. What part of our own schoolwork could be more exciting and enjoyable than this repetitive practice of *kanji*?

A second pleasure of *doing* that is equally central to the Japanese emphasis on repetition within learning is use of the *soroban*. Unlike the Chinese version of the abacus, this little instrument for calculation has only one wooden counter on the reed above the divider, four in the main section below it. The basic system is simple. At the beginning, all four of the lower counters are pushed to the bottom of the divided wooden frame, while the upper one is pushed to the top. In counting you first slide the lower counters up one at a time—*ichi, ni, san, shi*—then return them to their original position and bring the top one down for *go,* or "five." Continuing to count, you bring the bottom ones back up again—*roku, shichi, hachi, kyuu*—before pushing them back once more to their starting position and moving up the first of the lower counters on the row to your left, to indicate ten. Japanese children soon get dazzlingly fast at the *soroban,* not only for addition and subtraction but also for multiplication and division. Using their thumbs and index fingers for clicking the beads inward to the dividing bar, they often looked to me as if they were plucking a harp or banjo with a jaunty, rattling rhythm. This deftness stays with people in later life. Every bank clerk keeps a *soroban* next to the telephone. The shopkeepers in our part of Kyoto frequently used a long version of this instrument that, within a single plastic frame, had an electronic calculator on one end and a mini-*soroban* on the other. I've heard that it's faster to do multiplication, division, and percentages on the calculator, but that when it comes to adding columns of numbers the *soroban* is much speedier. At the elementary level, working with the *soroban* both makes children intimately familiar with the adventures of fives and tens and gives them the fun of a manual skill. If we're looking for transferable strengths from the Japanese educational system, I suggest we consider the advantages of such hands-on work as a way to focus children on mental processes.

Another of our big surprises in Kiyomizushō-gakkō was the rowdiness of the classrooms. We Americans have read about the pressures placed on Japanese high school students preparing for the "exam-hell" that will determine whether they are admitted to university. In our comparisons between Japanese and American education we also often refer to the suicides each year by teenagers who were unsuccessful in their exams. We console ourselves that their school system is as unbalanced, if in the opposite direction, as ours. But the truth is once more not so simple. Though the pressure on academically ambitious Japanese is indeed enormous, our neighborhood elementary school in Kyoto struck Rita and me as an extremely relaxed, high-spirited institution. When we walked down the faded grandeur of those lofty corridors, bringing in some necessary form or supply which we had belatedly found out about, we could hear the hubbub on all sides. One of our daughter's teachers in Vermont had once told her class that if they were in *Japan* they'd all be sitting attentively and taking notes instead of fooling around. But these classrooms witnessed chaos that would *never* be allowed in any American school I know about. Often when I stepped into one of our kid's classrooms at Kiyomizushōgakkō, I found about half the students out of their seats. Even if the teacher were presenting material at the board, there would be several other group-conversations going on in the room, punctuated by laughter.

But these are far from being dysfunctional class-rooms. The students simply start working collaboratively as soon as the nature of the new assignment becomes clear to them, while the teacher doesn't fret if the students don't hang on his or her every word. Part of what accounts for the jolly atmosphere in a Japanese classroom is the pleasure in group activity so essential to every aspect of the society. In addition, while the teacher's job is to *present* the new material, the students and their parents clearly have responsibility for *learning* it. At a supermarket where my wife and I sometimes shopped in the northern part of town, near Kyoto University, there was a section of manuals and practice books in every subject and at every grade level. Since the Japanese curriculum is entirely standardized, with sixth-graders all over the country learning the same things and carrying out the same projects on any given day, parents can confidently follow along in these manuals while helping their children to master their school assignments each night.

Because the students and their parents bear responsibility for maintaining forward motion with the basic academic skills, teachers are free to take a very flexible approach in the classroom. Rachel's sixth-grade teacher, Fujita-sensei, dedicated the last two weeks of the term to a collaborative art project by the class. It was a mosaic, about six feet by three feet, of Kiyomizudera, the ancient Buddhist temple from which the neighborhood and the school derive their names. Though not as well known to foreign tourists as certain Zen temples and gardens in other districts, it is one of the most famous Buddhist sites for Japanese—celebrated for its vast grounds, the waterfalls under which pilgrims stand (and from which it gets its name), and the lofty wooden columns that hold the temple's veranda up over a steep hillside. The sixth-graders' mosaic shows Kiyomizudera in March, just when they were creating their project. In the foreground is a cloud of pink plum blossoms, like the clouds that frame and exalt ancient Heian pictures of court life. Foliage and blue sky provide the backdrop, while the massive tile roofs and dark wooden walls of the temple fill the middle ground. Both the color sense and the execution of the mosaic are superb. To stand in the open foyer of the school gazing at it is like looking at a Seurat painting, a swarm of points out of which swims the world in all its depth.

Our children's experience of learning Japanese in the schools, as it turned out, had a *pointilliste* aspect as well. Having received no formal instruction in grammar, they had to pick up phrases wherever they could. Recognizing repeated patterns within familiar contexts was of the essence here, which made the playground an especially important place for their language learning. During games of baseball (using a tennis racket and soft ball), a strike would often elicit a triumphant shout of *Baka ja nai*, "Aren't you stupid!" If there was an argument or a contested point, they would settle things with a Japanese version of our rock, paper, and scissors game. *Jan ken hoi,* or "Let's make a fist," they would say, and then, if both kids made the same signal, *Aiko de shō,* "Draw! Do it again." Going over and over such sentence fragments, our children attained a level of fluency in Japanese that, while it didn't run to long sentences or complex structures, was both up to speed and completely idiomatic—two things that could never be said of my own command of the language.

On our last night in Japan we had dinner in Tokyo with the family from whom we had rented our Kyoto apartment. While the adults chatted, the children were playing or reading. In the middle of some game, Matthew and the Satōs' ten-year-old daughter launched into a boisterous round of *jan ken,* and our host wheeled around in astonishment at hearing a little blue-eyed American so perfectly reproduce the rhythms of a Japanese boy. Although the most close-mouthed little Vermonter among our three kids, Matthew had progressed so far into his new culture that he produced a sharp sense of incongruity in Japanese adults whenever he opened his mouth. When their classes had taken field trips around Kyoto, our children didn't even have to open their mouths to be incongruous. The students would all be wearing identical caps, of reversible red and white with thin elastic straps under the chin. But there would be one face in each class that didn't fit, causing people to do double takes on every train platform and in every museum. In a culture where uniformity and group identity are so highly prized, differences can feel like jarring dissonances. But the double takes registered connection as well as difference. An adult foreigner with the group, or even a little *gaijin* without the school cap, would not have been so startling a sight for bystanders.

One of the most interesting, and in its way pleasurable, experiences of living in Japan came in the tension between being included in more and more social groupings while never being viewed as any less foreign. As ardent baseball fans, we soon chose a team to root for during our time in Kyoto—the Hanshin Tigers. It was remarkably like the experience of being Boston Red Sox fans in our Vermont life. Not only are the Tigers the team of choice for the Kansai region, as the Sox are for New England, but they inspire a similar sense of doomed loyalty. Roger Angell has likened rooting for the Red Sox to backing the Trojans in Homer. On a good day they can beat anybody, but in the end they'll be done in by those big machines like the Greeks, the Yankees, and the Mets, or, in the case of Hanshin, the Yomiuri Giants. Sitting in the Tigers' Kōshien Stadium, reverberant like Fenway with the hopes of generations, we may have stood out as the only *gaijin* in the stands. But wearing our Tigers' caps of white with black stripes and a black bill, rising, sitting, and stamping with the chants, yelling through our little yellow Hanshin megaphones, and waving our Hanshin pennants, we were also enveloped by and contributing to the roar of fifty thousand equally deranged fans.

Because we were inescapably conspicuous, people in groups with which we became affiliated could more easily register our *belonging* as well. We soon became familiar sights in our settled and traditional neighborhood between the Kiyomizudera and Kiyomizushōgakkō. Two main groups lived there, the artisans who produced bamboo ware and pottery in the style called Kiyomizuyaki and the shopkeepers who sold souvenirs to the mobs of tourists coming to see the temple's famous plum and cherry trees each spring. The architecture of the district was yet another draw for this throng of mainly Japanese sightseers. Houses along those winding cobblestone streets have a number of distinctive features, including the so-called "cricket windows." During the Edo period groups of samurai would march up these streets on pilgrimage to the temple. People of the shopkeepers' class were forbidden to look at samurai from above. But the thin vertical slits of the cricket windows allowed them to look at whomever they pleased without being spotted.

Like Vermonters, who have also watched waves of tourists sweep through in season for many years, the people of Kiyomizu maintain an indelible sense of who are the locals, even on days when that makes them a minority. Hitomi, my conversation partner, once remarked that no matter how long *she* lived there, she would never be accepted by the people of that district. The fact that she came from Osaka would keep her from being considered a true part of the parents' organization at school or of any other neighborhood groups. Even had she only been born as far away as the southern part of Kyoto where her family and she now lived, that would have marked her to the Kiyomizu natives as a person to be held at arm's length. Her comments reminded me of a story told about the woman who moved across Lake Champlain from Port Henry when she was a toddler and spent the rest of her long life in Vermont. Her obituary in the *Burlington Free Press* is said to have begun, "New York Woman Dies at 93."

Because we were so much *more* foreign than Hitomi, we were noticed and, temporarily at least, accepted in a way that she and her children would perhaps not have been. When the neighborhood students donned special hats and coats to march around the temple behind a drum on festival days, our three were invited to join the procession. When we were preparing to leave for America, and buying some ceramics and bamboo goods to take with us, the shopkeepers insisted that we accept the local discount. Those marked, higher prices were for tourists, not for members of the community. And what above all had established that we belonged there, despite all outward appearances to the contrary, was the fact that, as the mothers of Kiyomizushōgakkō students went in and out of the school on their many errands, there were our kids, conspicuous as could be, but sitting at their desks or working on the art projects along with the rest of the gang.

Kiyomizushōgakkō represented Japanese education for us. But as we got to know people from other parts of Kyoto and from cities like Osaka and Hiroshima, we gradually came to understand that this school was an anachronism in certain ways that made it more similar to our schools in Bristol than to the pressure cookers of Tokyo. Even within Kyoto, which is approximately the size of Philadelphia, the Kiyomizu neighborhood is like an old-fashioned, self-contained village. The shops along the Kiyomizumichi that cater to tourists still thrive, and the teahouses and the *soba* shops still receive a lot of trade. But all over Japan the artisans' class is dying out, and the skilled ceramics and bamboo fashioning traditions of Kiyomizu are dwindling with them. The elementary schools of Kyoto's bustling suburbs often harbor a couple of thousand students within their low, characterless complexes. But the lofty classrooms and enormous playgrounds at Kiyomizushōgakkō contain only about three hundred. These are primarily the children of shopkeepers, since the artisans as a group are elderly.

One way this school resembles Bristol Elementary is that almost all of its students were born under the shadow of Kiyomizudera, just as in our town most kids in a given class have been together since kindergarten. Actually, in both towns it's likely that the parents as well as the grandparents will have gone to that school, too. This stability complements the central Japanese emphasis on group work, enhancing the meaningfulness of such collaborative projects as the sixth-graders' mosaic. I wonder if for such reasons our little school in a Kyoto backwater might not have been more characteristically Japanese than the up-to-date schools with their emphasis on individual preparation for exams.

The students at Kiyomizushōgakkō played after school and on weekends, like Bristol kids. My guess is that a fairly low number of them aspired to university. Instead, they would inherit their parents' shops and live in the apartments at the back of them. While avoiding the intense competition, the commuting, and the high housing costs that beset most Japanese today, they could still anticipate both a pleasant environment and a comfortable standard of living. Again, I'm reminded of Bristol, where there are relatively few college graduates or professional people, but where many people in the village live in spacious homes they inherited. It's not uncommon in our Vermont town for people to work at two jobs in order to make ends meet. But they live on tree-lined streets in a town with clean air and a crime rate so low that folks often don't bother to lock their doors, and where a number of century-old houses have never even had locks.

Though Kyoto itself is a big city, with a great deal of industry (including the Nintendo empire) and considerable pollution downtown, it has lent itself until recently to the settled pleasures of community. For almost forty years after World War II, the city was run by a popular Socialist mayor who believed in neighborhood high schools. Meanwhile, Tokyo, which dominates education as it does all other aspects of Japanese life, was developing its own elaborate and very different school system. Junior high students across that megalopolis take entrance exams, then attend the best high school to which they're admitted—best being defined as having the most success in getting graduates into Tokyo University and the other elite institutions. This system has meant that an increasingly high proportion of teenagers in the greater Tokyo area have commutes of an hour or more to school, either because they are traveling to a more selective school than the nearby one or because their local school is so competitive that they can't get into it. Such tracking also means that between their pressurized high schools and their *juku*, or private weekend cram schools, eighteen-year-olds from Tokyo generally perform better on standardized tests than Japanese from elsewhere around the country. Kyoto University is close to Tokyo in general prestige, and is particularly well known for its tradition in philosophy. But whereas in the 1950s a large number of the undergraduates there would have come from Kyoto, today an inordinately high number of the places in each entering class are taken by people who attended high school in Tokyo.

Under such pressure from outside, the tradition of community-based education is now breaking down in Kyoto. Here, too, the high schools are beginning to be differentiated according to the success in standardized exams achieved by their graduates, while numerous private schools are springing up that promise to help young people (and their families) study their brains out, despite living far from the buzzing hive of Tokyo. In America the experience of civic harmony is frequently restricted by the degradation of our public life. Those who can afford to do so often build walls around their privileged enclaves and pull up the ladders, while our downtowns and our public schools are abandoned to those who can't pay for a ticket out. Japan's momentum is in some ways just the opposite. Theirs is the triumph of public life. Wealth and technology have brought a new monolithic character to the traditional desire for consensus. But this means that *localized* values of harmony must now give way to ideals imposed from above by Japan's highly centralized bureaucracy. Bristol's Mountain Street School and Kyoto's Kiyomizushōgakkō are reminders of successful, but increasingly rare, experiences of community.

I realized, in preparing for this year in Japan, that I was drawn primarily to the culture's classical artistic and literary expressions rather than to contemporary Japan. What I hadn't anticipated, though, was the parallel role of cultural nostalgia in the children's *school* experience. Such nostalgia had to do in part with the small town quality of Kiyomizushōgakkō's neighborhood. When Rachel went through the graduation ceremony from sixth grade, at the end of the Japanese school year in April, almost all of the girls in her class were unconsolable. Holding their graduation bouquets in one arm, the girls leaned against the school wall or propped each other up in small groups, tears streaming down their faces. Going off to junior highs in other parts of the city, to which they would ride buses and where they would wear formal blue uniforms, they were stepping into the main current of Japanese education.

The old-fashioned school to which they could walk each morning along cobblestone streets, with the little store next to the gate where a bent *obaasan* sold school supplies and snacks, would seem increasingly just another dream of Old Japan.

The significance of the girls' tears, and of the place of an institution like Kiyomizushōgakkō in Japanese life, has something to do with the meaning of imitation in a traditional Japanese art like calligraphy. Just as this old-fashioned elementary school in a little backwater of Kyoto is marginal, an anomaly, so too is it culturally central. But as they become increasingly marginal and remote within contemporary Japanese life, the values of traditional art and community also become more clearly defined and precious. This is one of the most striking things about Japan today. Because so much in the current way of life is fast-paced and modern, traditional ways come to seem distillations of a more serene world into which people may dip for refreshment and reorientation.

When the new school year began in late April, my children had experiences that clarified the marginal centrality of Kiyomizushōgakkō for all of us. Rachel did not return to school. As her friends graduated and traveled to junior highs around Kyoto, we embarked on a program of home schooling with her for the rest of the year in Japan. One of the new activities Rachel and I undertook together was to enroll in a class on *nanga* painting. This is a style of watercolor painting, also called *suiboku*, in which brush, ink stone, ink stick, and paper are all similar to those used in *shodō*. The main difference is that translucent colors are added to some compositions.

Once a week Rachel and I would walk downtown for our afternoon lesson, through the cacophony of bus and taxi traffic, to our classroom on the upper floor of a mall that included several movie theaters. Going home afterward, we would stop for a slice of pizza at a wonderfully garish pizzeria dominated by plaster replicas of statues by Michelangelo and Donatello. But in the midst of all this cross-cultural flak the lesson itself was, once more, a serenely traditional experience. Our teacher would call students up to his desk and produce a painting for each of us while the whole group watched. We would then carry these models back to our own tables and start making copies for him to inspect and comment upon. With the exception of Rachel and me, all of the other students were women in their fifties and sixties, reimmersing themselves in the traditional arts now that their families were grown. Several were quite advanced in their skills, and worked on elaborate paintings of the famous temples and gardens of Kyoto. I spent my time on black and white compositions of the "four noble characters" of traditional *nanga* painting: bamboo, plum, orchid, and chrysanthemum. But for Rachel the teacher always had something special: evocative portraits of birds and animals, or, in one of our favorites, of a smiling, childlike pilgrim holding a staff and wearing an old-fashioned, shaggy straw raincoat and a broad pilgrimage hat.

Rachel delighted in copying these charming cartoons. I remember her adding the final touches of faint brown wash to raincoat and hat and coloring rosy circles on the little pilgrim's cheeks as our classmates gathered around her table appreciatively. *Kawaii*, they murmured, "cute"—meaning both the painting and the artist. But their pleasure was not just in seeing a little blonde American producing such a quintessentially Japanese painting. They might have initially focused on her because of her difference, but what they then saw was not a dissonance with their own culture so much as a harmonious enactment of it. In one of my last conversations with Narasaki-sensei when I stopped by the school to take him a gift of some *Uji Shin-cha*, spring tea made with the small new leaves, he made a revealing remark. He had been expecting that Rachel would be a "typical American"—by which I imagine he meant large, loud, and assertive! What he had found was a petite, rather shy student who also possessed an unusually refined aesthetic sensibility. In other words, she came remarkably close to a traditional Japanese definition of the feminine. Shyness is not necessarily a social or political advantage, in Japan or in America. But when it translates into quiet absorption in the traditional arts, it becomes for the Japanese an intensely attractive token of inwardness and sensibility—an echo from the murmuring richness of life in Genji's palace a millennium ago. The reticence and alertness that sometimes inhibit Rachel in American social situations, or leave her unnoticed by teachers or classmates in our noisy junior high in Bristol, made her seem to the Japanese who saw her painting or participating in a tea ceremony like a figure from the quietness and beauty of their own past.

Matthew and Caleb, too, experienced traditional Japanese culture in a particularly vivid and memorable way after the new school year started in April. A class on *kendō*, or Japanese fencing, began at Kiyomizushōgakkō on Saturday afternoons. The boys were initially excited by the glamorous uniforms—heavy cotton *hakama*, or wide trousers, with a quilted kimono, like the top of a *jūdō* uniform, worn over it—and by the practice sword. This sword was well over three feet long, the handle covered with suede and long enough to be held by both hands, the blade a tapering length of split bamboo that both softened the blows and made a satisfying crack when it struck. Along one side of this "blade" ran a taut red cord. A Japanese sword has just one sharpened edge, and this cord represented the unsharpened side, helping students remember their orientation while practicing various strokes.

One of our family rituals in Japan had already become watching a samurai show together on Saturday evenings. *Abarenbōshōgun*, or "Naughty Boy Shōgun," presented the adventures of a generalissimo who ventured forth in disguise from his castle near Osaka to mingle with the people and to defend widows, orphans, and the downtrodden. At eight o'clock, after the five of us had all had a chance to steam in the bath, we would pile up our *futon* in the central room and settle in for an hour of gorgeous costumes, spectacular swordplay, and feel-good plots that reminded me of watching shows like *Bonanza* with my own parents. The fighting in *Abarenbō-shōgun* was concentrated in the last five minutes, when the shōgun disclosed his identity to the villains and, first alone, then supported by one male and one female assistant, defeated them and their armies of retainers. There was never a drop of blood shown in these finales. Rather, the camera focused on the whirling choreography—the feints and footwork—as the shōgun parried and spun and as the trumpets blared out a theme song that sounded remarkably like Herb Alpert's "Lonely Bull."

Even within the shōgun's dazzling prowess, one could discern each of the strokes and combinations Matthew and Caleb were practicing on Saturday afternoons in the grand old auditorium of Kiyomi-zushōgakkō. The sword is so manageable, with two fists gripping its handle, that strokes follow each other in a staccato sequence like punches in boxing. During practice matches a student also wears a lacquered breastplate and a padded helmet with a sort of grate on the front like a catcher's mask. When the split bamboo meets the armor in a rapid succession of blows, a tumultuous din fills the air. Neither American schools and their physical education classes nor summer swim clubs and soccer clinics had ever offered our boys anything like this noisy, cathartic fun.

First, the more experienced students like Endō-san and Hashimoto-san would lead the group through

warmups and drills. At a word from them—
"*Men!*"—the other boys and girls would leap forward to pop their partners on the helmet and bounce
right back. Or "*Doh!*" would be called out, and the
students would feint from the left, then whirl the
bamboo sword around to hit the armor with a
slightly rising horizontal stroke from the right side.
After a few minutes the main teacher, Fuji-sensei,
would take over. He was a man in his mid-sixties
who had once actually served as the principal of Kiyomizushōgakkō. He had remained incredibly lean
and agile, and inspired our sons with his graceful
mastery. Knowing that they would only be living in
Kyoto for another month or two, he gave Matthew
and Caleb special attention, sometimes sparring with
them while the others were carrying out a group exercise. He would show them just which moves to
try, then help them to accelerate their speed by carefully regulating the rate of his own parries and coun-
terattacks.

Both Matthew and Caleb, barefoot on the wooden
floor with their teacher, and Rita and I, watching
from the doorway, had to laugh and shake our heads
at Fuji-sensei's wonderful speed and precision. But
the boys also sometimes came home with their heads
ringing, from the friendly whacks on their helmets
with which he followed up his parries. Singled out
by their status as visitors, but included by their uniforms and the drills through which they participated
in that synchronized community, the boys found in
kendō a culmination of their experience at Kiyomizushōgakkō. When each Saturday afternoon's prac-

tice was over, they would kneel in a line against one wall with all of the other students, swords and helmets neatly arrayed to their right. All of the boys and girls in the group would remain motionless and quiet for several minutes, to let the noise drain away, and to remember the discipline supporting the showy competition. Then, still kneeling, they would bow deeply to the teacher, as Fuji-sensei bowed back to them. This shared moment of silence, before all of those nine- and ten-year-olds scattered to walk back to their homes around the neighborhood, allowed the dissonance of individual effort to resolve into the underlying harmonies of gratitude and respect.

A
SHOWER
OF STONES

ON MONDAYS AND THURSDAYS I WOULD SET OFF for the Go club right after finishing my lunchtime bowl of instant ramen. After one block on Kiyomizumichi, the steep road that ran past our apartment-house door on its descent from the eastern foothills, I turned right and entered a network of cobblestoned streets. Quiet lanes wound north and west through our district of gift shops, teahouses, and the traditional inns called *ryokan*, eventually debouching into the park that surrounded the *Yasaka Jinja*. This Shinto shrine was invariably crowded with brisk, purposeful worshippers. They would stop by on their way to go shopping downtown or while on a break from work, toss a rattle of coins through the slatted tops of the wooden offering boxes, then pull on the ropes that rang bells around the edges of the shrine's roof. After clapping their hands twice and bowing they were finished, and strode out of the park toward the rest of the day's agenda.

On holidays the walkways around the shrine were

hung with illuminated paper lanterns and lined with carnival booths. I enjoyed strolling down with my children at such times, so that we could sample delicacies like octopus balls and squid-on-a-stick, or win prizes by firing at packs of cigarettes with an airgun. Even on days when no fair was going on, there would still be a few old women in the park displaying their goods on plywood counters held up by sawhorses. One vendor had a small but very choice selection of brushes, ink sticks, and ink stones. The one stop on my arm-swinging walk to the Go club was to look at her wares. Though I never purchased anything, she always had a friendly smile for me when I pushed off again.

Yasaka Shrine is at the corner of Shijō and Higashiōji (Fourth Street and Eastern Avenue) and marks one corner of Gion, Kyoto's geisha quarter. The geisha, and their apprentices the *maiko*, trip along through Shijō's crowds of tourists and businessmen, carrying their fans, wearing their high wigs, and dressed in the world's most beautiful fabrics. Everything about them is an exquisite balance of extremes. The faintest of colors, gold or mauve, are set off by astonishing lines of rich purple or green where the underkimono shows at neck and wrist. Heavy brocades largely obscure the women's figures. But the swirling patterns of these silks bring sensuality to the surface, drawing a passerby's attention to the only unadorned parts of a geisha's person—the long graceful hands carried at waist or breast and the double point of skin showing at the nape where white make-up has *not* been painted on, as a reminder of human flesh within the cultural artifact.

A Japanese friend had taken our family to see the *Miyako-odori*, one of those lavish productions where Kyoto geishas sing and dance to show which of their guilds is the most splendid. Within their venerable wooden home and theater, set in a large garden, women spoke to each other, and to the few men employed by them there, in familial address. It was a sisterhood through whose corridors we were escorted by a geisha whom our friend Mrs. Hayashi knew. This was their society, from whose solidarity of traditional dress and highly disciplined arts they ventured out, self-possessed and superbly eccentric, in their errands along the noisy streets of modern Japan.

I walked through Gion twice each week on the way to my own eccentric society. Turning north at the intersection of Shijō and Kawaramachi, I passed the principal department stores of Hankyū and Takeshimaya. Though much more up-to-date than the geisha, the people at this corner were always elegantly dressed, too, looking as if they had just selected their expensive clothes from the stores' racks. The men wore slimly tailored English suits, set off by furled umbrellas and by shoes with the soft gleam of Italian leather. With scarves highlighting their bold ensembles, the women looked more like Paris or Manhattan. I was headed toward a considerably seedier crowd.

After forging up Kawaramachi for five long blocks, I reached an unprepossessing little building on the left side. Above the third-floor window of its orange stucco front hung a sign with two large *kanji*. The upper one was the character for "surround," while the other combined the radicals for "basket" and "stones." Together they spelled *I-Go*, the formal name for the game more commonly referred to as simply "Go." Whenever I turned into the doorway and began to climb the Amsterdam-steep stairs, I was aware of hoping that some of the shoppers thronging Kawaramachi would notice me—a conspicuously tall *gaijin* in sweater and jeans, but one who nevertheless was walking familiarly into this private establishment on a street where most people were restricted to the sidewalk and the shops.

This was my club. I belonged here. Our smiling hostess always greeted me at the door, stamped my card, and brought me a cup of green tea. On Thursdays I often drank it while watching the teacher of our class finish up demonstration games with a couple of other club members. Okabe-sensei came over once each week from the *Kansai Ki-in*, the prominent Go club in Osaka that was the parent organization of our Kyoto branch. As the demonstration drew to a close I would gulp the rest of my tea and move into the back room where the class took place. I wanted to find a place near the center of that ten-tatami room, so that I could have a good view of the large magnetic board mounted on the wall with which Okabe-sensei guided us through a series of games each week. We students recorded them on special little pads, using pencils with red lead at one end and blue at the other so that we could more easily distinguish the "opponents" in a particular game. Okabe-sensei would judiciously click up groups of magnetized stones while discussing a particular variation, then suddenly sweep them all off the board with a grand erasing gesture. Most stones fell into the large wooden box in front of him, but others bounced off the tatami and were still rolling among us as he began to set up the next position.

Go belongs, with chess, to the category of "intellectual" games. These are the pastimes so complex that a person can invest a lifetime's thought and creativity in them, yet never stop discovering new possibilities. In its rules, Go is the simpler game. Onto a board with nineteen lines running up and down, nineteen running across, players tap down flattened circular stones of black slate and white clamshell. These pieces are placed one at a time on the lines' intersections, rather than in the squares, and once played are never moved unless captured by the opponent. The object of the game is to outline, then consolidate, territory in different portions of the board.

A game of Go quickly becomes more complicated than these few rules might suggest. For one thing, the two players' original sketches, or *moyō*, often overlap, generating intricately recursive contours from the straightforward lines of intention. For another, with a Go board's 361 intersections, compared with 64 squares in the game of chess, the range of possible moves is vast indeed. Go's enormous number of permutations accounts for the fact that, while programmers have taught computers to play chess at a very high level of skill, no Go program can beat even a moderately serious amateur. Its greater profundity has led to Go's replacing chess as the criterion for computer scientists trying to develop "artificial intelligence." Despite their formidable powers of analysis, even Go masters cannot comprehend an entire game in logical terms. They must also rely on their aesthetic faculties, responding to a configuration in one corner of the board with a stone in another corner just as a painter like Constable used touches of red intuitively to balance his enormous skies. Because of its challenges to the whole person, Go has traditionally been considered one of the four essential Zen arts of Japan, along with calligraphy, painting, and music.

In high school I was devoted to chess, with its spectacular struggles to control the center of the field. But, as I grew increasingly interested in Go during college, I was struck by the decentralized, ecological quality of its complexity. In Go there are *many* engagements around the board, and no single decisive event like a checkmate. Rather, the game ends quietly when both players agree that there are no more significant moves to make. Groups of stones will by then have achieved stable life in their various niches, large and small, through a surging, intricate accommodation like that of the biological community along a rocky shoreline. In chess there are fewer and fewer pieces as the game proceeds. But in Go the pattern of stones grows fuller and more complex, in a rich harmony envisioned by neither player yet reflecting every plan and effort along the way. Similarly, on the first afternoon when I mustered my courage to climb the steps of the Kyoto Go Club, my motivation was simply to become better at Go by playing people who were more advanced than I. This American strategy of self-improvement soon collapsed and exfoliated into a funnier and more satisfying experience, though—membership, as a foreigner, in a traditional Japanese club. Both my understanding of Japanese culture and my own sense of social identity were transformed by learning what such club life could mean.

By and large we students were a scruffy lot—who else would have devoted all those hours to playing a game while the rest of the nation pursued its efficient work? In my first weeks at the club, before enrolling in an afternoon class there, I encountered only men. There were a number of bristly retirees, whose wives had plainly told them not to come home before supper. A few journalists and professors came, too, professionals with flexible schedules, wearing proper dark suits but looking pretty rumpled in them and betraying in other ways that they were nobody's team player. For one thing, several displayed a fingernail about an inch long on the little finger of their left hands. Like my traditionally robed calligraphy teacher, these downtown types declared their allegiance to the culture of the literati. Regardless of the hustle and exhaust of Kawaramachi three floors down, they were pursuing the austere beauty, and the pure competition, of the world's most demanding game.

On one warm June afternoon a group of far-right patriots traveling in a convoy of trucks paraded on Kawaramachi. Songs, speeches, and chants blared from speakers on the roofs of the trucks, at a decibel level so high that it assaulted pedestrians' eardrums like a rock concert or a 747 taking off. The trucks' camouflage paint and the army fatigues worn by their drivers gave a militaristic jut to the cavalcade. Some vehicles flew the Emperor's chrysanthemum flag, while others displayed a huge map of Japan with the Kurile Islands, held by the U.S.S.R. since World War II, highlighted in angry red to the north of Hokkaidō. Many Kyoto residents feel both angry and embarrassed by these noisy, assertive demonstrations that tangle downtown traffic during the warm months. People had told me that they were organized by the *yakuza*, or "mobsters," who maintain their own successful society within the corporate structure of modern Japan. But despite the sound roaring into the open windows of our Go club, I was the only one who paid the slightest attention to the demonstration. No one else looked, commented, or otherwise diverted energy from a game. That was after all someone else's club and would not, for all of its brashness, be allowed to intrude into ours.

My own entry into the Go club, though not so noisy, had been far more challenging to everyone's equanimity. When I first walked up those stairs I was allowed to enter and play with no questions asked. All I had to do was pay the four hundred yen entrance fee and give another one hundred yen for each game I lost; if I lost three games it made for about a five-dollar day, the equivalent of two cans of Asahi beer. During the first several weeks I went, it was quite obvious that, as far as half the club's members were concerned, I was the invisible man. In part, this was because I was a *gaijin*, which in Kyoto means not only a non-Japanese but, just about as bad, anyone not born in this magnificent, jaded city. My Japanese was tentative, and I didn't know the basics of Go-etiquette—what to say when sitting down at the board, the right order in which to remove captured stones, the proper point at which to resign a lost game. My foreigner's ignorance was doubtless an irritant to the sense of *wa*, or "harmony," cultivated by members who climbed into this haven for many hours each week and had done so for years. But the most serious problem of all was the fact that I was simply not a very good player by Japanese standards.

Like many of the traditional Japanese arts, Go employs an elaborate ranking system. The *kyū*, or "amateur," ranks run from 35, the weakest, to 1, the strongest. Then come the *dan*, or "expert," players, whose levels *ascend* from 1 *(shodan)* to 9. And on top of those come the nine ranks of *professional dans*. Players at different levels of skill can still compete with each other, though, because of Go's traditional handicapping system. Before play starts, stones are placed on specified intersections around the board, with a stone being added for every grade of difference between the opponents. The best player I knew at home in Vermont was about 2-*kyū* in strength. When we played he gave me a three-stone handicap, reflecting the fact that I was about 5-*kyū*. Most of the regulars at the Kyoto Go Club were at least 1-*dan*, though, and a number were 3-*dan* or better. This meant that they would have to give me five to seven handicap stones in order to have a fair game. It seemed highly unlikely that I could teach them anything, I'm sure. At the same time, with such a large handicap I might just have won by playing conservative Go—a humiliating prospect, indeed. During my first weeks at the club people often made it plain that they would rather read or kibbitz over someone else's game than play me.

In Kawabata Yasunari's novel *The Master of Go*, there is a description of an epic Go match between an old master, who symbolizes the final flowering of Meiji culture, and a representative of the new Japan. At one point the journalist who is covering the match for a newspaper and who is the novel's narrator encounters an American on a train. The *gaijin* has learned the rules of the game and, though at 13-*kyū* he loses over and over to the narrator even with a six-stone handicap, he happily plays on. To the journalist's amazement, this American is totally unembarrassed by people gathering in the aisle to watch him lose: after all, it's just a game. The narrator reflects, "For him it was probably like having an argument in a foreign language learned from grammar texts. One did not of course wish to take a game too seriously, and yet it was quite clear that playing Go with a foreigner was very different from playing Go with a Japanese. I wondered whether the point might be that foreigners were not meant for Go."

A Japanese no more skillful than I would probably never have ventured into a serious Go club. I'm afraid that in returning doggedly during those first weeks I must have only reinforced the impression that I was a frivolous foreigner, like Kawabata's American on the train. But two events helped change my standing there. The first was finding a mentor, while the second was discovering the existence of the Thursday afternoon class and joining it. My sponsor was a dapper eighty-six-year-old, gold eyeteeth shining beneath the brown beret he wore indoors and out. At 4-*dan* he was one of the stronger players in the club, and at his age he felt no need to prove himself by beating other experts. When I first approached him, he seemed perfectly happy to give me a game. After being demolished in short order, I asked him in my most formal and polite Japanese, "*Oshiete kudasaimasen ka*," "Would you kindly teach me?" He cheerfully motioned for me to clear the board and prepare for basic training.

Like the other old gentlemen at the club, he spoke in broad Kyoto dialect, calling me and his other antagonists "anta," a form of "anata," or "you," that people from other areas of the country might find coarse or rude. While women from Tokyo were the easiest Japanese for me to understand, with their crisp articulation, higher voice register, and solicitousness for the baffled foreigner, these Go colleagues were by far the hardest. They delivered their fragmentary sentences in a gruff basso, laughing when I didn't get it but never doubling back. My old sponsor did at least act out some of the proverbs with which he was indoctrinating me. At one point early on, he told me that "Trying to win a game of Go by collecting a lot of small territories is like pissing rice." He)then delivered the message even more graphically by standing up and miming it, to the applause of everyone else in the club. Another time, when I had entered into a doomed struggle with him in one of the corners of the board, he said, "You're a sixth-grader and I'm a high school senior. Why do you always pick fights with me in dark alleys?" At that point he stood up and took a roundhouse swing at me.

This mock punch may have contributed to the nickname which registered the other members' first, grudging acceptance of me, *Amerika Champion.* It not so slyly acknowledged the two main problems with my presence in the club—foreignness and lack of skill. But it also signaled a change. People who'd never acknowledged my presence before began to come over and kibbitz when I played and gleefully to congratulate me whenever, having enjoyed a favorable handicap, my flailing Go overcame one of their cronies. In the boyish roughness that characterized this club, nicknames were the preferred form of address. Maybe that's why my kindly mentor had laughed at my bookish politeness. One distinguished, silver-haired gentleman I often saw at the club was rewarded for his elegantly youthful features with the title *Akachan*, or "Baby." As far as that went, my old friend never even told me his name until my last day at the club. He said that I should just call him *Ojiisan*, or "Grandfather." Whenever I addressed him in this familial way with my foreign accent it provoked another general laugh. But it also made a point about my beginning to acquire relationships in a society where, at first, I had been altogether out of it. I would describe my status in this transitional period as that of a mascot—like the giant, strangely colored chicken who amuses the fans in lulls from the main action at San Diego Padres games. At least people were getting used to seeing me at the ballpark.

This was the atmosphere in the smoky game room. Behind that arena, though, was a different world where Okabe-sensei offered his classes on Thursday afternoons. In that room, where we knelt on the tatami, shoes off, and bowed respectfully when the teacher entered, one felt the tradition behind our Go club's boisterous modern manifestation. At my *Ojiisan*'s suggestion I had eventually joined that class, even though it was on too high a level for me. Okabe-sensei treated me with exactly the same formal, scrupulous courtesy he offered to everyone else. And because I now had a recognizable and acceptable identity as his student, others at the club found it less baffling to deal with me. Another barrier was removed. Suddenly it seemed that everyone was willing to play me, everyone wanted to see me improve. I was one of them.

81

Wearing his elegant suit of fawn-colored Thai silk, Okabe-sensei would walk into the room with a pronounced limp that suggested childhood polio. Though he was dressed like anything but a monk, there was still an otherworldly austerity about our teacher. He combed his hair straight back, shining above his long, pale, introspective face. He was always good-humored during the lessons and really seemed to enjoy teaching. But at certain moments he would be lost to us in quiet concentration, gazing into the coalescing constellations of that giant board. Then, with a start, he would sweep it clear in a shower of stones that let the world begin again.

Okabe-sensei possessed the most phenomenal memory I have ever encountered. In graduate school one professor I knew had all of *Paradise Lost* by heart, and could recite, it seemed, from almost anywhere in Shakespeare and the Bible. But this Japanese Go teacher surpassed even those accomplishments. When Okabe-sensei instructed us at the magnetic demonstration board he used no notes, but simply referred to the thousands of games stored in his mind. He knew all of the classic games in Japanese history, all of the games played in major tournaments during his lifetime and, I believe, most of the games he had ever played himself. Further, he could walk through the club, scan the games being played by his students, then reconstruct them for us if they were pertinent to that day's class.

His memory differed from what we usually think of as photographic. It was keyed neither to words

nor to images, but rather recalled intricately unfolding patterns. In this sense it resembled *genetic* memory, in which forms are replicated through a gradual
organic process. Like the aboriginal people of Aus-
tralia, who can walk through a scatter of stones on
the desert floor and recreate their exact arrangement
days later, he needed neither to abstract nor to associate in order to remember. This comparison with
the Aborigines might seem incongruent, given Japan's high-tech, urban culture. But many of the artists, writers, and teachers of Japan would affirm it, I
believe. They are constantly asserting, "Remember,
we Japanese are not Western. We see the world
through different eyes."

When I describe my teacher's memory in genetic
terms, I'm thinking of his approach to Go during the
classes as variations on major themes. On one afternoon, he would look at patterns that might emerge
when an amateur, playing a professional, was given
a nine-stone handicap. On another, he might consider the variations emerging from a *jōseki*, or
"opening," invented in last year's Hon'inbō tour-
nament. Inevitably, he played simultaneously from
both points of view, each of his players making the
best moves appropriate to a particular level of skill.
I was reminded of the way in which Shakespeare fills
each character in his plays, giving each a center—
making his dramatic art at once impersonal and suf-
fused with emotion. Just so with Okabe-sensei's
demonstrations. We felt as if we were observing real
antagonists struggling on the board and at the same

time as if we were watching the orbits and eccentrics of the heavens from a cold, quiet tower. We transcribed each new pattern eagerly in our tablets, flipping our two-color pencils back and forth to keep up with his tidal memory.

When the class ended, he would return our bows and hobble carefully out of the room while we picked up the stray stones and straightened our cushions. Meanwhile he would be sitting at a table in the main game room, assigning us partners and handicaps for the formal games that followed each lesson. For the first two months I was consistently given the handicaps of a 5-*kyū* player. This meant that, after losing for several weeks, I began to win more and more frequently. But I wondered if my general level was improving and anxiously fretted for "promotion." Then one week he began to call me a 2-*kyū* and to assign my handicaps accordingly. This meant, among other things, that I was again losing more than I won.

Looking back, I think the reason Okabe-sensei avoided changing my handicap level stone by stone was exactly to discourage this hunger for improvement (the psychological equivalent of a growth economy). One of the benefits of a game in which there is usually some sort of handicap is that the players acknowledge right from the start who is better. There's no need to prove one's prowess at the board, therefore, and the real goal becomes realization of the game's potential for beauty, through collaboration in creating an environment beyond either person's plans. The game, rather than the handicap or the victory, is the thing.

At a temple garden in the north of Kyoto I once ran into a woman whom I had often seen as she was finishing her calligraphy lesson in the hour before my own lesson on Friday afternoons. Her session sometimes went on a little past the time for which I was scheduled, and I would sit quietly against one wall of the studio observing it. Having studied seriously for twenty years, she had developed a confident style of her own, and carried out cursive interpretations of classical poetry in characters so fluid that a novice like myself couldn't even decipher them. But in our conversation while walking around the garden she mentioned that our teacher had once told her that all his students were the same in his eyes. This meant, not so much that he cared equally for them, as that there was no significant difference in *skill* in his eyes. They were the students and he the teacher; he offered his art from his own center and they responded to it from theirs. What difference could there be? She said that in all her years of study she never forgot that comment. It had liberated her to be a student, without any need to compete or advance. Growth occurs when it is not the goal.

Reading over what I have written here about my Go and calligraphy teachers, I can recognize in myself a definite American type. Like so many compatriots I met in the streets of Kyoto, I was eager to be taught in the traditional Japanese way. The two men

I was fortunate enough to work with during my stay in Japan embodied this living tradition of masterly teachers. They were deeply skilled in their arts and benevolently focused on their students. But they also held themselves aloof from those students' personal agendas, conveying their traditions on a loftier and more authoritative plane.

You don't have to go to Japan to become aware how widespread the hunger for such a teacher is among Americans. When, upon returning to Vermont, our family watched the tape of *Teenage Mutant Ninja Turtles*, I recognized in Splinter the embodiment of a sensei-type prevalent in recent popular films. Miyagi-sensei of the *Karate Kid* movies is a similar conduit of Japanese (well, Okinawan) wisdom. As he tells his protégé about fighting from the heart and not using one's art for personal aggrandizement, he's teaching him too about the ancient Asian virtues of humility and respect. Obi-Wan Kenobi in *Star Wars* is yet another venerable warrior-sage, teaching an eager young samurai the spiritual outlook that will both perfect and transcend his physical skill. But the most interesting of these characters to me are Yoda, also from *Star Wars*, and Splinter. While both express idealized virtues and wisdom, neither is human. There is, it seems, a significant element of fantasy in Americans' desire for training from a foreign store of wisdom. We want teachers who really *know*, who are, in a word, *other*.

All of the cinematic senseis I have listed were adepts in the martial arts. At first that pattern seemed to correlate with the movies' large adolescent audiences, and to diverge from my own training in Japan. But then I remembered that *shodō* has been described by the Japanese as the ultimate martial art, a warrior's training in single-mindedness, with the brush as a sword. Go's military character is even more obvious, as opponents match strategies for controlling territory. Middle-aged pacifist that I am, it seems that I too have been drawn to the warrior's way, to the tempered self-control of the samurai, cutting away all that is not essential to the moment of trial. Robert Bly has written that, as women's identity has been blurred and devalued in the industrial West, so has men's identity lost a sustaining sense of intergenerational mission. Many men, he writes, need to enlist in some challenge that will test their mettle, if they are to escape the compulsiveness of a more infantile agenda.

This cultural legacy of solidarity and discipline is also related, though, to the striking social separation between men and women which a foreigner notices in Japan. My Go club was basically a male establishment, like so many of the institutions in Japan. Most of the *sararimen* ("salarymen") who toil in Tokyo's corporate headquarters go out drinking with their cohorts, including the boss, every night. This is a command performance, an expression of belonging to the clan. Often the men are also expected to have dinner together. This means, given the long commutes from business districts like Shinjuku to affordable housing, that they frequently have to spend weekday nights in special business hotels, where the rooms are cubicles stacked atop one another like berths in a train. Meanwhile *Kyōiku-mama* ("Education Mama") is running the home and putting in several hours on homework with her children each night. This extreme separation of the father from the family life has been recognized in a well-known wife's proverb of modern Japan: "The best husband is healthy and absent."

When I have been in restaurants or beer-halls where groups of *sararimen* were unwinding, however, I have always noticed that there were women standing by to help along the socializing of these workaholics. Waitresses kneel behind and slightly to the side of each customer in expensive restaurants, both watching that the right courses come to their particular charges and laughing appreciatively at the customers' jokes. These women take care of the men, as mothers would, and build up their sense of this being a special occasion. Just the same thing happened at the Go club. Until I joined the Thursday afternoon class, I never saw a woman in attendance.

In our small third-floor club, as in any Tokyo restaurant, there was, however, a hostess. This was actually the woman who *managed* the club, a cheerful soul with short gray hair and steel rimmed glasses who took our four hundred yen when we entered and led us over to one of the other patrons to suggest we have a game. Frequently, until she approached, the seated players would be sitting silently with eyes cast down, waiting to be tapped and brought to life. Then they would blink and motion the newcomer to have a seat. Before my *Ojiisan* offered his sponsorship, this was often the only way I could have persuaded someone to give me a game. As we began she would make sure each of us had a cup of fragrant green tea. Although I never saw her play or kibbitz, she was always aware of the games' progress. At the end she would be standing by the board with a warm smile, ready to collect one hundred yen from the loser and to hand the winner a piece of candy. Thanks, Mom.

Whenever our teacups emptied, the manager was ready with a refill. In addition, she circulated from table to table selling cigarettes. Almost every member of the club, like the majority of Japanese men I knew, was a heavy smoker. The air in the club room was thick. One warm spring day while I was walking by on Kawaramachi I looked up at the open club window and saw gray smoke billowing out in a cloud. My family, and especially my strong-minded daughter, hated this aspect of my visits to what they called the Cancer Pit. They made me peel off my smoky clothes as soon as I got inside our apartment, scrub thoroughly, and climb into a steaming bath. By the time I had soaked for a while in water up to my chin, most of the contaminants had been removed, and I was allowed to join everyone else in our living room / dining room / kitchen. This bath provided, among other things, a symbolic demarcation between my little male society and family life.

Many of the people I played on my two afternoon

visits a week themselves came every day, from the opening at ten o'clock until dinner. While a Japanese championship game will last for twenty hours, extended over two days, and while my own games in America had generally run between one and a half to two and a half hours, these seasoned Kyoto amateurs often finished a game in twenty or thirty minutes. Unlike the top professionals, they were not breaking new imaginative ground. Very often the opening and middle game would play itself out in variations they knew by heart. They were really plucking dozens of memorized moves out of the air at a time, click-clicking the stones back and forth, then pausing to choose the next module. My *Ojiisan* loved building straight lines in his game, seemingly without regard for whether they were on the inside or the outside of his opponent's formations. This meant that he was about the fastest player in the club. He would grin as he placed the next stone in its totally predictable place in line, daring his opponent to ignore it. As the game neared its end, he would either neatly consolidate his central *moyō* or, if he had been running along inside on the third line, artfully invade the center, destroying the other person's territory.

One of my other favorite antagonists happened also to be an older gentleman who wore a beret. He was neither so old nor quite so skillful as my *Ojiisan*. But he still played at a 1- or 2-*dan* level, and impressed me with his admirable vagueness. While *Ojiisan* was a jolly bricklayer, this man scattered his stones in a white cloud around the board. He was impassive and silent while we played, then, win or lose, would beam when the game was over. I have a clear image of him rising slowly from the board at five o'clock each afternoon and hobbling down the stairs bent over his cane so that his daughter, who was waiting at the sidewalk, could drive him home.

On Thursday afternoons women came into the club as players, sheltered, as I was, under the umbrella of Okabe-sensei's class. Of the eighteen of us who regularly attended that class, four were women who carpooled up from their homes in one of the southern suburbs. They were in their late forties, part of a generation just beginning to break into the male solidarity of establishments like this one. I think they must have felt even more conspicuous than I in the club, and they certainly gave the impression of keeping their heads down. They were very serious about their Go and were undoubtedly encouraged by the fact that Okabe-sensei treated them with the same scrupulous, impersonal courtesy he accorded to the Japanese men and to the lone *gai-jin* in the class. The atmosphere in the tatami classroom was much less intimidating than that in the main club, too. We sat on the floor, with no talking except when one of us was addressed by the teacher, while the boisterous fraternity met elsewhere.

One woman was a stone or two stronger than I, and with the handicap assigned me I beat her in two of three games we played. She seemed truly chagrined by this. Looking back I can understand this reaction through the nickname that she had received even before I had my own—*Onna no Hito no Champion*, or "Women's Champion." As with mine, but even a bit more pointedly, the name both acknowledged her growing skill and took her in and, at the same time, put her down. To lose to a *gaijin* was not what she had in mind, and she was clearly neither eager to chat nor willing, unless assigned to do so by Okabe-sensei, to play me. She had a friend, smaller, grayer, and older, who was not in her class as a Go player and was actually one of the few players a couple of stones weaker than I. Whenever we were assigned to play, therefore, I gave her the handicap and had the unusual experience of taking the white stones. And, all three times, she won. Each time she reversed our fortunes very near the end, either killing one of my groups or rescuing one of hers that I had thought done for. She exulted in these triumphs and happily called her friend over, along with others who, in passing by earlier, may have assumed I had a won game.

Her exuberant celebration turned my own good-loser's smile a bit wooden. I was feeling something akin to her friend's emotions at *my* two victories over *her*—embarrassment at being seen to lose to someone who was, as I was, marginal, both weaker than others in the club and "different." So easily can snobbishness grow from the memory of being shunned. Despite such strained moments, this woman and I maintained a congenial relationship, along with anticipation of the next contest. One week in the summer, shortly before our family's scheduled departure from Kyoto, she asked me about my other activities in Japan. When I told her of my pleasure in studying calligraphy and also about my class in *nanga* painting, she exclaimed that she shared these same interests. Then Okabe-sensei walked into the classroom and our conversation came to an end. But when I arrived for my last day at the club she had a present for me.

It was a large flat box, filled with rolls of the finest quality paper, both for calligraphy and for painting. It also included a couple of brushes, a nice stick of *sumi* decorated with a floral design in gold leaf, and, at the bottom, several of her own paintings. This present touched me more than any other I received in Japan. Its generosity and its aptness were moving, as was the inclusion of her own art. Beyond that, I felt in it the acknowledgment of a bond. We were fellow lovers of the game and classmates. But beyond that we were people who pursued our interest in Go at the periphery of the club's social circle. We thus belonged to a smaller club within the club.

My Go teacher, too, had presents for me. I was astonished, because I had never been sure how much, in his dreamy, distant politeness, he had really noticed my presence in his class. One of his gifts was a handkerchief from the *Nihon Ki-In,* Tokyo's preeminent Go club. Printed on it were "Go proverbs," such as "Capture the cutting stone" and "Don't approach thickness." The other was a fan with *kanji* elegantly brushed onto its plain white surface: "Quiet observation ultimately prevails."

This was Okabe-sensei's final word of advice to me. Be patient. Instead of launching desperation maneuvers, remember the guiding principles of the game and play with serene concentration that goes beyond winning and losing.

My *Ojiisan* was there to say goodbye on the last day, too, looking as spunky as ever. We exchanged cards in Japanese fashion, and I saw with surprise that his name was Korean. He was a senior, respected member of the club and, from his broad Kyoto dialectic, might have been a native of that city. But he was nonetheless a member of Japan's most sizeable ethnic minority. Koreans in many cases are visually indistinguishable from Japanese even to the Japanese themselves; they often speak flawless, unaccented Japanese; and in some cases they have even taken on Japanese surnames. But they are not allowed to assume citizenship and are resolutely held outside the elite circle of Japanese business and government. Though they are not necessarily conspicuous through skin color or other racial features, they are treated consistently and negatively in terms of their race, no less than any minority in Europe or America. I suddenly realized that my *Ojiisan* had taken me into the club, sponsoring me when others were dubious about my presence, in part as a way of reaching out to a fellow *gaijin*. In this final conversation he asked where we were going after we left Japan, and I told him our family would be traveling to Hong Kong and Thailand. "Why don't you try to work in a visit to Korea, too," he suggested. "It's a great country."

I still carry around in my wallet the *Kai-in-shoh*, or "membership card," from my Kyoto club. In addition to the three large *kanji* on the central line, for "club," "member," and "certificate," it is closely printed with other characters. I decipher them one at a time now, as if studying corner positions in a game of Go, then try to compose them into a whole game. There are the characters for "capital" and "universal," spelling Kyoto. Then come the *kanji* for *hombu*, or "headquarters," and the ones for *I-Go*. Looking at those radicals for "basket" and "stones" reminds me again of the container into which Okabe-sensei splashed magnetic pieces at the end of each illustrative game. Superimposed on all this printed information are various ink stamps—the large red chop of the club, the black stamp showing my participation in the "Thursday class for intermediate level players," and the little red circles recording each of my monthly tuition payments. On the very top line is my name, printed neatly with our hostess's black ballpoint pen. It is definitely the place any Japanese eye would immediately go if asked to spot the giraffe in this picture. Whereas their names would be in *kanji*, mine is in *katakana*, the syllabary alphabet used to approximate foreign words and names. *Jyon Erudah.* Certainly not a Japanese name, but not standard English either. It's the name of a foreigner who belongs to a Japanese club.

INHERITING THE INVISIBLE

THE WIFE OF THE DRUMMER FUJI, VISITED BY A DIS-
turbing dream, has set off for the capital with her
daughter. She arrives just as an official is announc-
ing the murder of her husband by a rival drummer
named Asama, who had been invited to play a concert for the Emperor Hanazono and who became
jealous when Fuji, too, came to play his drum at
court. The dead man's robes are brought out to his
widow, who stands there swaying with grief. Not
quite knowing what she's doing, she begins to put
them on. Her hands, hidden within the voluminous
sleeves, clutch her husband's drumsticks. In a dance
that starts very quietly, she furls the sleeves around
the sticks and unfurls them, first one and then the
other, with circular motions of her outstretched
arms. As the spasms of her suffering grow more intense, she begins to beat her husband's drum. She is
bitterly striking the instrument that caused his
death. But at the same time, dressed in his robe, she

has become the drummer Fuji. Her grief is a haunting, as the dead man's spirit possesses the body of his living wife.

The dance from *Fuji Daiko* conveys the essence of Japan's Noh theatre—the ghostly persistence of vanished lives. A Noh play often has very few lines and even less action. The audience must come already familiar with the story, so that the actors, by their subtlest gestures and movements, the quaver of their voices, and most of all the quality of their stillness, can evoke its heart. Playing Fuji's wife in the performance of this play we saw at Tokyo's *Kanze Noh Gakudō* was our friend Uzawa Hisa, an actor with reason to be especially aware of the mysterious continuities within her haunted art. Her father Uzawa Masashi is a Noh actor designated as a National Treasure by the Japanese government, and she is attempting to perpetuate his art within this most remote and interior of the world's dramatic traditions. Though Betchi, as our friend is called off stage, has studied with other famous teachers and has now been a professional for twenty years, she has always remained mindful of her father's elusive mastery. His is the robe she has put on, so that the spirit of the dance may pass into her. Her life's work, as she once said to me, is a project of inheriting the invisible.

Betchi has been made keenly aware of transition and continuity within her ancient art for another reason: she is one of very few women to establish herself in Noh at the highest professional level. Despite the facts that her father is renowned as an actor, that her mother also is prominent in the arts, as a well known instructor in *ikebana*, or traditional flower-arranging, and that Betchi herself completed a degree at the prestigious Tokyo University of Fine Arts while studying Noh privately, she received little encouragement to continue in her chosen field. Even her father at first discouraged her from going on to become a professional.

The most persistent suggestions made to Betchi after she had determined to pursue Noh were about appropriate times to quit. Her graduation from the university and her marriage were two moments when acquaintances were sure she'd give up her strange ambition. When she later had a daughter, the event struck them as an even more fitting time to stop. Then, when the birth of a child did not have the desired effect, they suggested she now have a *son* and quit. On the Sunday afternoon we attended the production at *Kanze Noh Gakudō*, her ten-year-old daughter Hikaru was also on stage in *Fuji Daiko*, playing the daughter of the character played by Betchi. Hikaru's was the *Ko-kata*, or "supporting role," in the drama. Her mother's part was the *Shite*, or "doer," the principal actor who dances the dramatic moment that is narrated, in turn, by another supporting actor called the *Waki* and by the chorus. The watchful poise of Hikaru's small figure on stage sharpened the event for the audience. Like the rest of us in that theatre, she was witnessing the migration of a spirit—simultaneously into the wife of drummer Fuji, into the career of her mother, and into a new tradition of female Noh actors in which she too will have a part.

The second play on the afternoon's program was *Ōhara Gokō,* or "The Imperial Visit to Ōhara." This time Uzawa Masashi was featured in the *Shite* role as ex-Empress Kenreimon-in, at the period in her life when she has withdrawn in seclusion to the Jakkō-in temple in Ōhara. She has seen her Taira clan destroyed by the Minamoto at the naval battle of Dan-no-ura. A Minamoto soldier prevented her from drowning herself, but not before her mother and her son, the boy Emperor Antoku, had both leapt from the ship to their deaths. The play is set in 1186, one year after the battle, and relates the retired Minamoto Emperor Go-Shirakawa's journey from the capital in order to visit Kenreimon-in and to hear her story.

In the play's first act we see Kenreimon-in setting off to gather flowers in the hills around the temple, along with a former lady of the court who has withdrawn from the world with her mistress and has, with her, become a Buddhist nun. In its second act the retired Emperor arrives at the temple and encounters the returning Kenreimon-in. He hears her describe the course of her life in the Buddhist terms of karma and delusion, then relate the circumstances of her son's death. The program we were handed upon entering the theatre contained this description of *Ōhara Gokō*: "The play has extremely little action. Kenreimon-in's movements are almost entirely restricted to her entrances and exits; there is not even the final dance found in another static work, *Komachi at Sekidera*. The play is nevertheless filled with an unusual poignance, not only because of the beauty of the language but because of the situation: an empress, now dressed in the severe habit of a nun, recalls the death of her son and the destruction of her family."

I'd gone out to eat with Uzawa Masashi in the noisy Oden restaurants of Tokyo, where patrons yell out their orders and waiters slam and slide the dishes along rough trestle tables. He loves such hearty local fare and easily holds his own in the bustle of elbows and voices. But now on stage this sturdy man in his seventies is transformed into the tragic figure of the empress. On his face is the *waka-onna*, or "young woman's," mask. In the fashion of Heian Kyō, as ancient Kyoto was called, small eyebrows are smudged high up on the forehead of a smooth, impassive countenance. Each of Uzawa-sensei's movements in this, one of his celebrated roles, is intensely feminine, from the tiny steps that make a glide of walking to the subtly shifting position of torso and hands, registering tides of emotion that sweep over Kenreimon-in but never destroy her composure or her courtesy. The feminine, as Japanese culture has always understood it, is above all a highly cultivated *style*. This stylization attains its apex in the rich falsetto cultivated by Uzawa Masashi within his *waka-onna* mask. His vocal range on stage is basically that of a contralto, with an exaggerated but perfectly controlled vibrato making the lines throb and veer from tone to tone.

Once, when visiting Betchi at the Tokyo house where her father and she also offer Noh lessons, I wondered if I might take a picture of her in costume. She excused herself to change from the sweats in which she'd been practicing earlier that day and returned in a few minutes dressed in a dark, formal robe and carrying a couple of the wooden masks which are heirlooms in any established Noh family. One was an old woman's face, its pronounced cheekbones and the lines beside the mouth suggesting the haggardness of long suffering. The other was a *waka-onna* mask, over a hundred years older than the first and one of the Uzawas' most valuable possessions. There was a smoothness, almost a blankness, to the features beneath the ancient patina of this mask. It represented the freshness and vulnerability of youth, thrust suddenly into the violence of a people's massive, unsettling history. Betchi posed for me displaying this mysterious *waka-onna* mask about chest high. Her fingertips were pressed lightly against the contoured wooded sides, as if holding a photographic plate at the edges in order to avoid smudging it.

In my photograph, Betchi's own face is centered above the wooden mask, and is equally impassive. She wears no makeup and keeps her thick hair in a short, no-fuss cut. It's a face as far from the high feminine style of twentieth-century urban Japan as from that polished countenance of Heian Kyō. A Westerner on the streets of the Ginza or Shinjuku districts of Tokyo notices how many women wear high heels and heavy makeup, affecting a sort of dressy glamor much less common in America since the fifties. Such emphasis on the artifice of beauty goes along, for a visitor from abroad, with another striking effect. This is the exaggeration of gender within vocal range. Men tend to speak at the bottom of their range and, especially in conversations within their working cohort, to favor a jocularly gruff, monosyllabic style. By contrast, women speak in very high voices, often using the most polite and in-gratiating forms of address. To hear these little-girl voices coming from mature women can be discon-certing at first, though it soon becomes positively associated for a visitor with the extraordinary atten-tiveness through which Japanese hostesses make their guests feel at home. The best equivalent that I can think of in our own culture is the traditional Southern Belle, her identity indistinguishable from the ideal of charm. But in Japan the model feels at once more extreme and more pervasive. One begins to realize the considerable effort it must take to pro-ject one's gender so unceasingly. One Japanese woman who has lived abroad for decades told me that she rarely returns to her homeland any more because she can't bring herself to "chirp."

I was first exposed to some of these issues when undertaking the study of Japanese in Vermont. My extraordinarily gifted and demanding teacher was a Japanese woman who was married to an American and who had been teaching in the United States for a number of years. A foreign-language teacher often tries to convey some sense of the texture and feel of the culture from which that language has emerged, and which has been shaped by it. I was struck, in occasional reflective pauses within the press of studying *kanji* and memorizing dialogues, by Endō-sensei's ambivalence as an interpreter of Japanese culture.

She drew attention to the fine nuances within forms of address, insisting right from the start that we recognize the subtle decorums of Japanese. And, in introducing us to *kanji*, she was careful to note the poetic richness of these characters—tissues of sounds and words growing around ancient hieroglyphics. But it was also evident that certain aspects of her own language were an irritant to her, reminding her of frustrations she had faced as a woman in Japan. She would point out to us that men in the dialogues frequently used blunt and unadorned forms and said that if the language was that rude you always knew it would be a man speaking. In the *kanji*, too, she saw a male-centered perspective transferred from T'ang and Han Dynasties China to Japan. An example she pointed to was *kanai*, the word with which a man would refer to his own wife. The constituent characters were "house" and "inside," which Endō-sensei combined and translated as "the woman in the back of the house." When she was growing up, our teacher had felt confined by gender roles that were reinforced every time she spoke. Teaching us Japanese in Vermont, an ocean and a continent away from Tokyo, she could still taste that world on her tongue.

In social conversation, though she is very friendly, Betchi makes no effort to raise the pitch of her voice into the register of charm. On the other hand, when she dons the *waka-onna* mask and takes the Noh stage, she pulls her voice resolutely *down,* to match the quavering contralto that issues from the small oval mouth-hole of that mask when her father performs in the same roles. Behind the mask, within the low voice to which she has schooled herself, she impersonates a male actor impersonating a woman. In June of 1988 she first wore a mask as a professional on one of Tokyo's most important stages. That event was the culmination of seventeen years in the profession during which, although she possessed the very highest credentials and was already making a name for herself as a private teacher, she was only allowed to work backstage. It had been a dramatic test of her patience, or perhaps a standing invitation to go away.

Betchi chose to take it as a trial, and to pass it, knowing that she would never leave unsatisfied. And in fact, though she was clearly being held off stage because she was a woman, some such testing has traditionally gone on in most Japanese arts. Students who traveled to a pottery village to study with a famous potter were first given a broom. After a year of sweeping, perhaps they would be allowed to help in mixing the clay and, a year or so later, if they had not yet stormed off in frustration, would finally be allowed to begin shaping it into vessels. Betchi's ordeal surpassed any such tale, but was still an aberration in length rather than kind. In fact, because her training was so protracted, it could also be considered particularly traditional.

Having tempered her art for seventeen years, Betchi was ready from the moment she stepped onto stage to command it with a confidence that removed all questions about her right to be there. And, unlike male Noh actors of her generation to whom well-established paths opened more readily, she has also found it natural to consider where her tradition might develop further from here. "Internationalization" is one of the buzz words in Japan today. Japanese feel that their new economic dominance calls upon them to enter more fully into dialogue and exchange with other cultures. This means, among other things, that there is an impetus to bring the literature, art, and music of Japan more widely into world culture. Such forwardness is uniquely hard, though, for a people with one of the world's most insular histories. As Edwin Reischauer points out, Japan is considerably farther away from the Asian mainland than Britain is from Europe. And for two centuries during which many countries were being transformed by the industrial revolution, the Tokugawa shōguns chose, in the interest of political stability, to isolate Japan almost entirely from foreign contacts.

Beyond such factors of geography and history, Japan's difficulty in pursuing "internationalization" may be connected with the essentially Confucianist character of her traditions. Each traditional art is a mountain-seat of authority toward which students must toil. It is a shrine, not a road show. When I asked Betchi about Noh's capacity for reaching out to foreign audiences, she said that this would have to happen through women actors like herself. While it is essential that Noh actors have the highest degree of professional training, Betchi believes that a man with such a background would have so identified himself with the discipline of imitation that any rethinking would be nearly impossible for him. A woman who, despite her skills, had long been held at the margins of the Noh world could take a view of the art at once concentric and eccentric.

Betchi's sense that women will need to lead the way in imagining a future for those same Japanese arts that have traditionally excluded them seems right as one surveys the artistic scene. Though the musicians of Japan, for instance, have often mastered western modes of composition and performance, an impulse toward genuine cross-fertilization with traditional Japanese forms has been more likely to come from the West. One of the nearly countless examples is Benjamin Britten's *Curlew River*, bringing a Noh drama into the tonalities of opera. I have noticed a similar lack of symmetry in the various formal Christian-Buddhist dialogues at which I occasionally find myself. Often, these conferences come down to American Christians saying, "We're eager to explore ways in which your tradition can help us to reconstruct our own," and Japanese Buddhists saying, "We've got a few minutes. Ask away."

American eagerness for the new—as opposed to Japanese self-containment—is a well-established aspect of our culture. We've even coined a term, "frontier mentality," to characterize our readiness to move on, to try another life, to seek out the margins. This may partly account for my experience, as an American man, of special affinity with Japanese women. They are both one with Japanese culture and ready, with me, to look at it from the margin.

My conversation partner in Kyoto was a woman who had spent two years in Minneapolis while her physician husband was carrying out a post-doctoral fellowship at the University of Minnesota. Their middle son, now about eight, was born there. Once a week we met at my family's apartment near the Kiyomizudera to exchange an hour of conversation in Japanese for one in English. The note I'd found posted by her on the bulletin board of the International Community Center had stipulated that she'd prefer a woman for such an exchange. But I called her up anyway, and she decided to give it a try. Over the months of our conversation we became friends, and toward the end of the Japanese sojourn our two families went on several picnic outings together. Such socializing with the entire family was definitely an American custom rather than a Japanese one and reflected the couple's experience in Minneapolis. Nevertheless, Hitomi's husband, like most professional men in that country, did work remarkably long hours, constantly presenting research papers in Japan and around the world and frequently missing dinner with the family.

My own life could scarcely have been a more idyllic contrast. I spent most mornings studying *kanji* and luxuriously reading through Basho with my dictionary. The big events of my day were afternoon outings to gardens with my wife Rita or visits to my Go club and calligraphy teacher. Conversations with Hitomi frequently turned to these enthusiasms of mine, and I'm sure that I must have seemed a full-time hobbyist. At one point when I said jokingly that I probably worked less than any man in Kyoto, she assured me that I must work less than any man in *Japan.*

Hitomi and I met initially because she wanted to practice her English and I to learn more Japanese. We soon discovered an equally strong and mutual desire to follow up on the personal sense of connection we felt with each other's culture. During my family's time in Japan I was aware of the fact that many experiences, aesthetic and personal, felt deeply meaningful and utterly foreign at the same time. Hitomi's years in Minnesota had left her with a similar sense of baffled and sympathetic curiosity.

When we compared Japan and America we naturally tended to praise each other's countries, both out of courtesy and because temperamentally we were enthusiasts. I continually remarked upon how good it felt to be safe in a big city. Not only in Kyoto, but in Tokyo of the ten millions, a man or woman can walk through the downtown at any hour of day and night without fear of street crime. Japan has a negligible drug problem compared with ours, and one finds few homeless people. Hitomi, for her part, admired the value placed upon creativity and personal initiative in our culture. Even a sabbatical like mine, in which an institution supported a teacher's enriching adventure outside his main area of work, represented the American culture of possibility for her.

One of my reactions to daily life in Japan surprised and amused Hitomi. This was my delight in the grand courtesy with which customers are greeted in Japanese places of business. I loved this aspect of my visits to the Bank of Kyoto, whenever I walked over to our branch office on Higashiōji for the weekly withdrawal from our dwindling account. At the moment I walked through the door all of the clerks sang out, and I mean sang, "Yoku irasshai-mase," "Welcome!" When I left a few minutes later they would loudly chorus, "Arigatō gozaimashita," "Thank you very much!" Even though these were just conventional courtesies, their vigor and volume also convincingly expressed to me both appreciation of their customers and a sense of shared purpose in advancing the business of that bank. For Hitomi these shouts were old hat, no more exciting than a taped "thank you" from one of the vending machines on Kawaramachi.

In a similar way, many foreigners before me have been entranced with the hieroglyphics within *kanji*, seeing a dance of little figures within the script. For Japanese, who have used it almost all their lives, a character like *suki* is much less likely to resolve into the constituent pictures of a woman with a child. It is simply the symbol to represent the adjective "good" or the verb "to like." Perhaps all cultures need outsiders—whether coming from abroad or emerging from groups in some sense at the margins of the society—to return to the origins and make the tradition new.

My interest in Zen was also not shared by most Japanese whom I got to know. An American visiting the great Zen monasteries of Kyoto will indeed find them treasure houses of painting, sculpture, and architecture. But there is little sense of connection to contemporary culture. These monasteries seem essentially museums, with the priests often serving as curators or living history guides. This effect would be inevitable to some extent because of the press of tourists, including the spring throngs of junior high classes from all over Japan. But it also has to do with the fact that, in many of these *zendos*, there is no longer regular sitting. Smaller Zen temples scattered around Japan look back to these famous founding monasteries as their headquarters, but they too have come to play a less vital role in Japanese society. Most temples support themselves (and very well, too) as funeral parlors. Shinto is the presiding genius over births and, along with an added layer of Western gowns and perhaps even a ceremony in a Christian church, also oversees weddings. But most Japanese still call upon Buddhist priests for their funerals. Perhaps there is a symbolic sense that this religion, with its central emphasis on transience, is the closest to death. These little neighborhood tem-

113

ples are often handed on from father to son, with the inheritor traveling to a monastery in the same lineage for training but not necessarily continuing with the practice of sitting meditation *zazen* after returning to take over the business. So a Zen temple in Japan can resemble a lucrative car franchise in America, and indeed the large, expensive cars in the driveways of neighborhood temples become familiar landmarks for those who like to stroll through historical neighborhoods.

One of the things I've always valued about America is the adventurous mixing of genes and family histories that occur in marriages within our diverse population. My Scotch-Irish grandmother, with her north-Louisiana twang, and my wife's north-Italian grandmother, who immigrated as an adult and never quite learned English, might have seemed to have little in common beyond their red hair. But across the gap of two dark-haired generations their genes have met in my red-haired son Caleb. This is the disclosure of unsuspected and, to me, dramatic kinship, and is related to the promise of connection between cultures as different as America's and Japan's. On the surface, our two countries might seem to have almost nothing in common beyond a passion for baseball *(yakyuu)* and an obsession with personal hygeine. But, bound ever more closely together by our economies, we may also now discover that coming to terms with each others' differences can help us renew our own traditions within a complex process, sometimes aggravating and sometimes comical, of cross-pollination. Zen, through establishing practice centers in America, may be able to escape both from its imposing history and from its corporate prosperity. Similarly, in Japan, where Christians make up less than 1 percent of the population, the "nonchurch movement" has taken Christianity beyond the denominational divisions and church-building obsessions sometimes besetting it in America. The Japanese church has offered important leadership in such areas as refugee affairs. Like Betchi in her isolation within Noh tradition, Japanese Christianity has found rich new possibilities in its persistence at the margins of society.

The ground floor of the Uzawas' house is largely given over to a full-size Noh stage. A walkway leads around the stage from the front door and vestibule to the kitchen and family room at the rear. One Saturday afternoon I sat on the tatami at one end of the stage with Kobayashi Michio, an engineer with Tokyo Electric who was a student of Betchi's. She had asked him to come in and tell me about Noh, since from 1966 to 1968 he had worked for General Electric in Schenectady and was fluent in English. Across the stage, two of Mrs. Uzawa's *ikebana* students had set up a narrow platform and were working quietly on their floral arrangements. On the stage itself Betchi, wearing a formal robe, was leading one of her other students, a young woman wearing jeans and a green velour top, through the movements of a dance suggesting combat with a lance. Each of them carried a stage lance of unfinished wood, five or six feet in length, thrusting and sweeping it to punctuate the moments of stillness and define the angles of memory.

Kobayashi-san and I were watching a videotape of a Noh production with the volume turned low while he gave me a commentary on both this particular play and the art's larger significance in Japanese culture. *Ataka* takes its name from a place in northern Japan where, near the end of the twelfth century, a famous encounter took place at a checkpoint erected by the Minamoto army. The commander of the Minamoto, who had recently crushed the opposing Taira forces in a series of decisive battles, was Yoritomo. But his younger brother Yoshitsune, who was beloved by the people for his beauty and nobility as well as for his valor, was really the warrior who had won the day. The jealous Yoritomo decided to kill Yoshitsune and eliminate potential competition. The action of *Ataka* takes place at one of the numerous checkpoints Yoritomo has set up in order to trap and destroy his fleeing brother. Yoshitsune is traveling with a small band of retainers, including the folk hero Benkei, a giant of a man who is absolutely devoted to his captain. They have disguised themselves as *yamabushi*, or "mountain priests," with Benkei leading the way and Yoshitsune following toward the rear of the procession, carrying the pack of a porter.

Togashi, the samurai lord in charge of the checkpoint, is suspicious enough to quiz Benkei upon his priestly status and mission, but the old warrior bluffs his way through. Then Togashi catches sight of Yoshitsune's noble form at the end of the line and is about to halt the party. Seeing this, Benkei pretends to fly into a rage at this laggard porter and beats him soundly. Given the reverence of true retainers for their masters, and the legendary love of Benkei for Yoshitsune, such treatment is intended to eliminate any possible suspicion about Yoshitsune's true identity. And indeed, after this outburst, the commander of the barricade simply waves the party through. The emotional core of *Ataka* is not in anything the principals do, however, but rather in its aftermath within each character's soul. It is subtly but clearly indicated that Togashi saw through Benkei's ruse, but was so moved by that warrior's willingness to sacrifice his own deepest feelings in order to save his master's life that he pretended to be fooled. Benkei, for his part, is staggered by grief at what he has had to do. When they are past the checkpoint he begs forgiveness of Yoshitsune, who grants it, weeping with him at the sadness of such a world.

It is characteristic of Noh's indirection that the retainer's sensibility should be central to the play, while the famous warrior prince is played by a child and speaks his lines in a high piping voice. Characteristic, too, that the action is repeatedly broken by moments of dead silence—as in the sudden pause after a line of gorgeously robed knights slowly wheels around on stage, or after the staggering sight of a servant beating his master. Those silences are the imagination's openings, when the emotional reverberations of the story pulse into the audience's heart. As Mr. Kobayashi said several times while we watched the videotape, "Silences are very important in Noh." They define the space within which an audience can reestablish contact with traditional Japanese attitudes. Central to the tradition, for Noh, is an emotional tone, as captured in the redolent word *Kadensho*, with its roots in the *kanji* for "flowers," "transmission," and "book." Flowers because, behind all of the wars and personal tragedies of their history, Japanese perceive a natural cycle of blooming and withering that roots humanity in nature. In the Western tradition this insight has been expressed in the biblical reminder that "All flesh is as the grass," while Bashō remembers Yoshitsune's career in the haiku "Summer grasses, / all that remains / of soldiers' dreams" (*On Love and Barley: Haiku of Bashō*, trans. Lucien Stryk, Honolulu: Univ. of Hawaii Press, 1965). The sense of a larger natural context for both military glory and personal anguish is reinforced by the musicians at the rear of the Noh stage, moaning and yelping as they drum, playing the flutes in a wild wail that suggests nonhuman passions on distant mountaintops or in the depths of the sea, where whales commune with songlines far beyond our metronomes.

The videotape was of an amateur production staged at Tokyo's lavish National Theatre by Uzawa Masashi's advanced students. The musicians were professionals, though, while Uzawa-sensei and Betchi, wearing dark clothes, moved along the back of the stage changing props and setting up the scenes. They were the *kō-ken*, or "watchers from the back."

Yoshitsune was represented by Betchi's daughter Hikaru, then seven years old, her shrill, clear voice ringing across the stage while her mother and grandfather silently crept back and forth arranging for each new scene. At the back of the stage rose the wall where, as in every Noh theatre, a single windswept pine tree was painted. Its broad, twisting branches and blue-green tufts of needles were the only backdrop. This was the tree of Noh, rooted in a history of grief—awakening generations of Japanese to the spirit underlying and ennobling daily routine, carried into a new world where I watched from the tatami as Betchi and her student swept their feet across the wooden floor, stamped, and wheeled around in a traditional reversal of the lance.

WHALEMEAT

An unanticipated benefit of having our children attend Kiyomizushōgakkō was the hot lunch they were served there every day. We had been startled by the high price of food in Japan, so that when Rachel, Matthew, and Caleb returned from school that first week describing the huge bowls of rice they helped carry up to the classrooms from the kitchen, the fish or prawns served with it, and the cartons of milk all around, we began to hope that we might just be able to afford this year after all. But one winter's day our children came home unhappy about the stew they had been served. They had consumed their bowls of food before realizing what that red, chewy meat was, then were distressed to learn they too had now eaten whale. A Japanese friend from Tokyo was amazed when we told him about this incident, not because of the ethical or political controversies swirling around whaling, but simply because he found it hard to believe a neighborhood elementary school had actually served something so *expensive*. The fact

remained, though, that even with whalemeat running from thirty to seventy-five dollars per pound,
the school authorities had made the decision to ex-
pose Japanese children to this traditional food. For
Japanese and Americans alike, Japan's decision to
continue whaling is a symbolically charged fact. It is
also an area in which even sympathetically inclined
citizens of our two countries often have a particularly hard time understanding one another.

The Japanese aesthetic of nature has enriched my
own terrain for me since our family's return to Vermont. Hiking along the spur of the Green Mountains which lies to the east of our village, I perceive
the woods differently for having walked the temple
grounds of Kyoto. In Vermont, too, we have rock
gardens. Each winter, frost heaves boulders up out
of the bony soil that drove so many settlers west
after the Civil War and turned the hill farms back to
woods. Beeches bend their roots around these rocks.
Red oaks, toppling in high winds along the ridge, lift
up half-circles of interwoven roots, with stones as
big as loaves or basketballs exposed among them,
glinting in the new light.

Stone walls and abandoned cellar holes keep being
tumbled by the respiring earth, too, until they sub-
side into the elegant scatter of the garden at Ryōanji.
Like that celebrated garden's fifteen stones, these
relics are ringed with moss. The rhythm of gray and
green, dry and wet, leads an onlooker into a cycle of
perception as fruitful and mysterious as the genesis

of soil. The gardens I admired in Kyoto were designed in the period between six hundred and two hundred years ago by artist-monks who derived much of their inspiration from the tradition of black-and-white landscape painting originating in southern China. The compositions scattered through the woods above our Vermont village date both from the much longer history of geological collisions along this ridge and from the relatively recent convulsions of settlement and emigration in this state. But the Japanese gardeners' eyes have nonetheless helped mine to recognize an elusive order in woods where they never walked, to discover a natural value unintentionally parallel to theirs.

The Japanese tradition of sensitivity to nature has often intensified our Western experience. Japanese poetry, architecture, and gardening, as well as cabinet-making, paper-making, and textiles, have been powerful influences on present-day culture in America and Europe. An appreciation of asymmetry and of natural forms and textures has been helpful to Western artists wanting to escape from closed or geometrical design and from the oppressiveness of heavily worked or sealed surfaces. Japan's poetry, where natural details have not been subordinated to the ego and its logical propositions, has also become a chosen tradition for many writers around the world, just as the Zen which influenced haiku poets like Bashō has become a point of reference for environmentalists who want to abdicate the Western sense of patriarchal warrant of dominion over nature.

But over the past couple of decades, many of those

Westerners most attracted to the Japanese tradition of nature have been surprised, distressed, and increasingly outraged by the rapacity of Japan's exploitation of the natural world. In part, the environmental destructiveness of Japanese practices reflects that country's economic growth. As their economy has come to rival and, in some important regards, to surpass that of the United States, so too have the ecological disasters perpetrated on the world by Japanese become similar to those enacted by us Americans. Like ours, theirs is an oil-driven economy, with a standard of living, according to a recent United Nations report, higher than ours. And, as a manufacturing giant with few natural resources, they have become ravenous for the materials growing on or lying beneath the surface of other lands.

Beyond the major threat posed by their manufacturing machine to global forests and the atmosphere, though, Japan has also isolated itself dramatically as the nation most resistant to the elimination of whaling. In 1981, when the International Whaling Commission (IWC) voted twenty-five to one to institute a moratorium on sperm whaling, Japan's was the sole dissenting vote. They persisted in hunting sperm whales until 1988, even though that species was endangered. And although in that year they finally acceded to the IWC's 1982 moratorium on all commercial whaling, they have exploited a loophole in the IWC document that allows limited whaling for "research" purposes. Annual sales of meat from the hundreds of Minke whales brought home by Japanese whalers under this program amount to billions of yen.

Japan's persistence about whaling has done much to tarnish that nation's image in Europe and the United States, especially given incidents like the collision between one of their boats and a Greenpeace vessel during a recent Antarctican whaling season. In view of the facts that international trade is the basis for Japanese wealth, and that, with their scarcity of natural resources at home, they are particularly vulnerable to anti-Japanese backlash among world consumers, it has been hard to understand why the government has been determined to protect a whaling industry which makes up so minuscule a fraction of their nation's fisheries.

The question of why Japan should take such an inflexible stance is a troubling one. On the surface, it seems to have little to do with economic or political self-interest, and on a deeper level it appears to violate the sensitivity to nature that has always been one of the principal elements of Japanese culture. For us in the West, especially those of us with a sympathetic interest in Japan, it thus represents a source of confusion as well as a conflict. As an environmentalist and a nature writer, I find myself asked how I can square my own continuing enthusiasm for Japanese culture with that nation's continued whaling.

One simple yet significant fact is that the Japanese like the taste of whalemeat much more than most

Europeans or Americans do. The Japanese Whaling Association ran a survey which reported that 80 percent of the respondents wanted to eat whalemeat, while 70 percent said that commercial whaling should be continued. A common statement, as reported by the surveyors, was that people liked to include whale in their diets because Japanese had done so since ancient times. The fact that Americans don't generally eat whalemeat and Japanese do thus affects our differing views of the whaling moratorium. Perception is always colored by desire, as seen in the conflicting views of antismoking ordinances often held by smokers and nonsmokers.

A recent statement by Japan's representative to the IWC expressed anger at other nations' "ethnocentrism concerning food habits." He went on to argue that Japan should be granted special permission to take and eat whales, just as certain Eskimo groups in Alaska are allowed to continue taking bowhead whales for their own villages' consumption. This analogy between remote villages in Alaska and the economic and technological juggernaut that is Japan would strike most non-Japanese as ludicrous. But I believe that it may accurately reflect the Japanese self-image of being both isolated and culturally distinct, as well as a people for whom, despite all outward signs of economic dominance, subsistence is a daily concern. In this regard, the way Japan clings to whaling resembles its insistence on subsidizing domestic rice farmers, even though people could eat much less expensively if American and Thai rice were allowed to come readily into their markets. If there were ever a nation that lived by trade, Japan is it. But in such highly symbolic areas as whaling and rice farming, at least, they want to control their own destiny.

In some ways, the Japanese intransigence about whaling is simply the most dramatic example of a general resentment of foreign interference in Japan's economic and political systems. The aggravation many Japanese felt about the recent trade talks with the United States focused on one point: in order to continue with the international commerce that the Japanese economy requires, they were being forced to rearrange their domestic system of distribution. From the Western point of view, this is simple fairness—cutting through the web of middlemen who effectively seal non-Japanese goods out of the market. For the Japanese it means substituting bigger stores for the numerous, tiny neighborhood operations that have made big cities feel more like villages and that have often supported the elderly. It is a hateful imposition on their Japanese ways of doing business.

It's important to recognize that, despite the surprise and distress of Western environmentalists, neither Japan's appetite for whalemeat nor its desire to maintain national sovereignty come into essential conflict with that culture's traditional love of nature. Rather, they accord with distinctively Japanese beliefs about the spiritual and aesthetic meaning of the physical world. At its heart, the Japanese love of nature is microcosmic. This fact is evident both in the garden at Ryōanji and in many little details of modern life.

On a street near our apartment in Kyoto was a shop specializing in local spices and condiments. Different blends were packed in individual sections of bamboo, with a little wooden plug to be removed for shaking some of the mixture out onto a steaming bowl of noodles. In one of the little showcases the shop owner displayed a venerable bonsai tree. Half of it was a plum, the other half, grafted onto the same trunk, a cherry. It was old, to judge from the gnarly bark, even though the total height of tree and branches was not over eighteen inches. The bonsai was planted in a rectangular ceramic container, flat and green. When the plum trees on our street bloomed, so did the plum within the window. The blossoms were as big as those on the full-size tree, but looked much larger on those boughs no thicker than a chopstick. There was a week, as the cherries in Maruyama Park were just beginning to flower, when the tree in the shop window was full of pink-purple plum blossoms on one side and cherry blossoms, white with a tinge of pink near the center, on the other. Then the plum faded into its leaves and the cherry held the stage of spring.

The Japanese have always loved art that magnifies the small, from bonsai to haiku, by identifying the particular with the universal. They have discovered within local expressions the largest forces of nature. There's another side to this: the same dynamic has allowed Japanese culture to control those vast forces, to make the large small. The intensity of response to nature has derived its sharpness from the often frightening face of Japanese nature over the centuries. Tsunami have swept the coastal villages. Earthquakes have tumbled down houses, despite an architecture of wooden posts set on stones to maximize the buildings' flexibility and their capacity to absorb shock. Given the traditional building materials of wood, paper, and straw, Japanese homes have always been particularly vulnerable to typhoons and fire, as well. Wherever they looked, the Japanese have seen forces threatening to eradicate their settlements.

It seems to me that eating whales may actually typify the pleasure of rendering the vast and fearsome small. Cubing a whale for stew, or slicing it fine for *sashimi*, is the most striking reduction of scale, and hence the most impressive demonstration of control. Eating is, on a symbolic level as well as a physical one, a process of internalization. This metaphor of digestion and absorption is much more central to the Japanese vision of nature than it is to the Western view. We in America, especially, take pleasure in the notion of "wilderness." Our Wilderness Act of 1964 uses the adjectives "pristine," "vast," and "untrammelled" to distinguish such wilderness from the settled landscape. The value of such terrain is taken to be its separateness, a place over against human culture where people can go to escape our social roles and experience the world on a different level. Wilderness, from such a perspective, is the wild heart of nature.

By contrast, the Japanese find intense natural pleasure through enfolding nature within history

131

and culture. Bashō took special enjoyment in visiting scenes his poetic model Saigyo was associated with, just as that twelfth-century predecessor had planned *his* travels so as to see places visited by his own hero Kukai over three centuries before that. A Zen garden like the one at Ryōanji is walled in on three sides. On the fourth is a wooden viewing platform, from which one looks into the garden as into a painting. In this way, the garden continues the tradition of Sung Dynasty paintings, where the artist and his friends entered imaginatively into the mountains and forests of the ink and paper, wandering in the image and then returning refreshed to mundane reality. Art and nature, venturing forth and pulling the world back into oneself, become in this fashion indistinguishable. On the one hand, such an attitude has guarded against the dichotomies between spirit and matter, subjective and objective, by which Western culture has been plagued. On the other, it may contribute to the apparent difficulty the Japanese are experiencing today in grasping the reality of extinction or to the heedlessness with which they, as a nation rooted in the worship of trees, are depleting the world's forests. Just as we in the West need the delicacy and integration of their natural celebrations, they need, perhaps, a sense of nature more *separable* from their own sensibilities and microcosms.

There must be continuing international pressure upon Japan to give up whaling. It may already be

WHALEMEAT

too late to stop the blue whales and sperm whales from drifting into extinction, but we must try, much as we have tried, apparently successfully, to restore the population of peregrine falcons in the eastern United States. Such commitments to the survival of other species, like the development of a wilderness ethic, are basic tests of humanity's capacity for maturity and humility. They are important indications as to whether we will finally be able to survive in a healthy, balanced biosphere. But we in Europe and America must realize that in asking Japanese to give up whaling we are asking them to make what they feel to be a radical change in their cultural practice. Are we prepared to undertake as fundamental a critique of our own preferences in food?

In John David Morley's novel *Pictures from the Water Trade* (1985) a young Englishman sits in a bar sampling tiny red slivers of whalemeat. His Japanese comrades are concerned about the Western furor over whaling, and they ask this Westerner why killing whales for meat is any different from killing cows and pigs. He replies that cows and pigs can be bred, while whales cannot. It's a good answer, as far as it goes, but does not address the morality or the ecological consequences of our non-Japanese choices about food—the sorts of questions that the Japanese rightly raise given the sort of pressure now being brought to bear on them. American practices of feedlots, animals injected with hormones and antibodies, and egg factories where chickens never touch the ground are pretty hard to affirm as alternative "traditions" of food production. More to the point,

133

the American taste for fast-food hamburgers, now successfully transplanted to Japan, is a major influence in destroying the world's rain forests. Hundreds of thousands of acres are being bulldozed in order to raise the beef for our drive-through lunches. Are we prepared, then, in asking the Japanese to give up their eating preferences and a measure of their national autonomy, to sacrifice some of our own antiecological habits? For that matter, if we are truly serious about forcing an end to whaling, can we bring ourselves to carry out a boycott that might mean giving up some of the ingenious and delightful electronic devices which we so avidly buy from the Japanese? The 1984 bilateral agreement with Japan suggested that we were willing to weaken the whaling moratorium because of our own perceived trade interests. Unless we demonstrate a willingness to sacrifice, we can scarcely expect the Japanese to regard our outrage about their whaling very seriously.

Finally, Japan and America alike are called upon to reinterpret our traditions and revise our practices in relation to the natural world. One irony of the recent trade tensions and of the conflict between our two countries over the issue of whaling is that precisely in our traditional love of nature we have much to offer one another. In both countries there has been a collision between a powerful tradition of natural sensitivity and a rapacious, technology-driven economy. It is not so much that we have lost our way as that dangers inherent in our cultures from the start have been disclosed by our new power to bend the physical processes of the earth to our desires. The emergence of America's National Park system, the development of our wilderness ethic, and the growth of the genre of personal, reflective nature writing that flourishes in the United States today are all inextricably related to the industrial boom that began after the Civil War. In Japan, too, sensitivity to nature has often been entwined with less benign social facts.

Flower-arrangement, poetry, the tea ceremony, and landscape architecture, those arts through which the Japanese love of nature has been so strikingly expressed, all reached new levels of refinement under the Ashikaga shōguns in the fourteenth and fifteenth centuries. Visiting the Gold and Silver Pavilions in Kyoto one is reminded of the exquisite sensibilities of their builders, the shōgun Yoshimitsu and his grandson Yoshimasa. Yet under the Ashikaga the people of the city experienced nothing but misery. Plague and warfare ravaged the city as the shōguns shut themselves up within their gardens, planning new and even more splendid artistic endeavors. The love of nature in microcosm was a hermetic pleasure for them, and was no more attentive to the sufferings of the people then than it has proven to be to the plight of the whales today.

But Bashō, in the latter part of the seventeenth century, showed another way to appreciate the microcosmic arts of nature. Although he too was a lover of the tea ceremony, gardens, and painting, Japan's most famous poet imbedded his haiku in a life of traveling the length of Honshū. Rather than acting out a selfish fantasy of refinement and immortality, he pushed out along the road in all weathers, experiencing his own frailty and discovering compassion for other creatures, human and nonhuman alike. One of our challenges, in all of the industrialized countries, is willingly to accept more discomfort in our lives, rather than destroy the atmosphere and water through the pollutions of our hermetic transportation and living arrangements. Bashō welcomed discomfort as a bond with other forms of life:

> *Early winter shower—*
> *Even the shivering monkey wants*
> *A straw raincoat.*
>
> (trans. R. H. BLYTH)

We are entering an era in which those of us in the industrialized world will have to give up some of the comfort which so much of human history has devoted itself to attaining. This is a very difficult road to double back on. Only because the suffering of our planet, including millions of the human victims of drought and famine, is expressing itself more and more clearly can we even contemplate such change. The microcosmic love of nature may also offer one source of strength and consolation now, allowing us to bring into focus saving forces that have been blurred in the larger devastations of our landscapes. An artist like Bashō suggests how we may integrate such moments with a passage outward into sympathy with other forms of life.

Models are available to us in the Western tradition, too. St. Francis, recently declared the patron saint of ecology, has been proposed as a corrective to Genesis's emphasis on "dominion." His was a comprehensive view of nature, finding sisters and brothers throughout creation. Our American ancestor Thoreau can help us as well. In *Walden* and his other writings he suggests the limitations of an abstractly transcendentalist view, which holds nature to be simply a staging ground for human thought and spirituality. Thoreau says that we need instead to "have intelligence with the earth." In the confusions of wealth and power nations need, not to abandon traditions, but rather to enter into them more fully, following the examples of the poets and authentic spiritual leaders. At such a time Americans, like the rest of the world, can also continue to draw strength from the traditional Japanese vision of nature. After all, whales, enormous as they are, are themselves microcosms, capturing in their pulsing mystery both the chemistry of the sea and this evolutionary moment when all of humanity is challenged to expand our sense of identification and responsibility.

WILDNESS
AND
WALLS

I TRAVELED SLOWLY TOWARD JAPAN, THROUGH A
landscape of literature, observing the beauty of each
new season as it flowed into the life of the people.
Lady Murasaki, in the eleventh-century *Tale of
Genji*, slid open the door disclosing a garden of
Heian courtiers. Her shining company played their
flutes under the moon in time to the swaying of the
bamboo. They dyed the bamboo of those flutes to
match the green of the pines and dressed in the "wild
aster combination" as fields around the palace gave
way to magenta and green. Six centuries later, in the
time of the shōguns, Bashō walked north toward the
bay of Matsushima, "the pine islands." Looking
over that world of wind-sculpted rock, of trees bent
out over the thousand coves, he composed a haiku in
which the Japanese name gusted into the rush of
water, of wind:

> *Matsushima ya*
> *aa matsushima ya*
> *matsushima ya*

141

The more I read, the more I wanted to follow Japan's testimonies of natural freshness back to the landscape of their origin, to experience a sensitivity to the earth transcending the dichotomies of the American wilderness movement. The American system of national parks, culminating in the Wilderness Act of 1964, had made a unique contribution to the stewardship of nature in the twentieth century. But it had also contributed in certain ways to the polarization of "nature" and "culture." At any rate, that phase of our environmental evolution seemed to have come to an end with the passage of the Alaska Lands Bill in 1980. I wondered whether the Japanese perception of a natural harmony that included humanity might now help Americans become more attuned to nature within urban and suburban settings.

On my initial visit to Japan in May of 1987, when I finally laid the books down and boarded a plane for Tokyo's Narita Airport, a visit to Bashō's Matsushima Bay was one of the first items on my itinerary. I took the Shinkansen, or Bullet Train, north from Tokyo to the coastal city of Sendai, then transferred to the local that carried commuters and tourists out to the bay itself. Since the poet wrote, Matsushima has been celebrated as one of Japan's three most beautiful landscapes. My route from the station to the harbor was marked by plastic statues of the poet, posted along the sidewalk and featuring the large, bulbous nose that is his trademark. But wherever I stood to look across the water—from the ridge of an island attached to the mainland by a long footbridge, from the teahouse constructed on shore by the *daimyo* Date Masamune, from the Zuigenji Temple on the high ground farther inland—the view was dominated by the enormous smokestacks of a power plant. Not only were they far taller than any other natural or human form along the coast, but the tops were encircled by commanding red and white stripes. As the tour boats, their prows shaped like the heads of peacocks and dragons, cruised out through the islands, it seemed that they were bearing straight for these overwhelming verticals.

Even with all the careless "development" that is a fact of life in America, it seemed shocking that the Japanese would allow such a monolithic eyesore to be constructed at the focal point of one of their most revered natural and cultural sites. In the following weeks, however, as I traveled around the country with my Japan Rail Pass, I saw major construction projects just about everywhere I went. Even when taking a ferry to Hiroshima through the Inland Sea, I was rarely out of sight of a derrick on the shore, or out of sound of earth-moving machinery. The nineteenth-century prints celebrating this coastal landscape hovered in my mind; I looked through them, as through faded transparencies, at the gray emerging face of the new Japan.

Arriving in Hiroshima, I was taken out to dinner by several friends of a Japanese colleague of mine. We sat on tatami mats around a long, low table in the restaurant's upper dining room, relay after relay of Kirin beer loosening our tongues. One man, a professor at Hiroshima University, shared my interests in Japanese and American literature. As the conversation with him bobbed and turned, there came a moment when I could ask the question that had been growing in my mind. Could the love of nature so distinctive and central to Japanese culture survive the current boom of building, industrialization, and natural exploitation?

With no hesitation, Professor Aihara answered yes. Take a stroll down any alley in Hiroshima, he advised me. Beside the doorways and in the windows I would see lovingly tended bonsai trees, set out to take the morning air. Or for that matter, he said, look down at the platters on our table. Tiny raw octopus were bedded on seaweed, looking just as they had when they were netted that morning. Chrysanthemum heads were arrayed around whole prawns and lightly grilled whole fish. Such meals celebrated the forms of nature; they were daily experiences of communion. Professor Aihara went on to remind me that practically every Japanese name derives from natural objects, that the graceful strokes of traditional calligraphy, too, grow out of the twining lines of grass, the drooping curves of willows. Nature was not just the background of Japan's culture: it was its heart.

I knew that these examples were true to the Japanese tradition. Bashō's poems offer *moments* in nature, not landscapes in the conventional Western sense. In my favorite of his haiku, a single raven on a bare branch hones the edge between seasons—*aki no kure* ("the fall of autumn"). The Ryōanji garden of Kyoto is another distillation of this microcosmic genius. A rectangle of fine, light gravel is surrounded by walls on three sides and enclosed by an airy meditation hall on the fourth. Fifteen rocks of varying size and shape are scattered down the length of the rectangle, a number of them rising out of thick clumps of moss. Though mature trees tower above the walls, the rocks and gravel, in their mysterious balance, become the onlooker's whole world. Some people have discovered in this arrangement a mother tiger leading her cubs across a stony riverbed. Others have seen an ocean in the ripples of raked gravel, with islands, or continents, rising up from the mossy surf. If one sits long enough on the hall's long wooden steps, though, this dry garden gradually conveys the more resistant, more refreshing integrity of *wildness*. Thoreau writes in *Walden*: "Nature puts no question and answers none which we mortals ask. She has long ago taken her resolution." Since the fifteenth century, this ten-by-twenty-four-meter plot has offered to monks and visitors alike the unresponsive resolution of nature herself.

The architect Ashihara Yoshinobu has pointed out in his book *The Aesthetic Townscape* (1983) that the Ryōanji garden, while separated from the surrounding landscape by its walls, is not meant to be viewed by a person standing inside it. Its balance and significance are available only when one is sitting within the temple building looking out at it. This follows from the special status of the floor as a "sanctified" space in a Japanese building. Ashihara writes: "It is from this elevated position inside that the landscape outside is intended to be viewed." Two

145

details of Japanese culture confirm his distinction. One is the verb that describes entering a house, a tea cottage, a temple: *hairu*, or "to go up." The other is the fact that one always leaves one's shoes at the door, and with them leaves the dusty mundane world.

I recognize another version of Ryōanji's ironic separation and enclosure within the walls of my experience. In Go, the corners of the board offer the areas which are easiest to control; thus, the opening of a game frequently becomes a contest to see who can dominate in them. But a strong player will sometimes prefer to place stones outside the corners. Giving up secure territory for the sake of what is called "outside influence," such a player begins in effect to wall in the center of the board. I have always loved this reference to the *inner* part of the board as the *outside*. Like looking at a Klein bottle or a Möbius strip, it bends my mind around. This paradoxical language also feels natural, though. Moving inward from the edge leaves a certain security behind. Aesthetically and psychologically, it is a venture out, into a landscape of potential.

But I'm still not sure Professor Aihara's "yes" was right. I spent a morning at Ryōanji, sitting on the long wooden veranda beside the garden. Every half-hour or so, a bus would pull up and a school group would bustle around the temple grounds. Again and again, a boisterous knot of blue-uniformed teenagers would walk out onto the platform and begin to count the rocks loudly. It's hard to take in all of the garden from any one vantage point, and the kids would usually stop with a laugh when they got to eleven and race off to the next building in the compound. The students seemed to be having a great time and were certainly neither noisier than American youngsters on a similar outing nor less attentive to the morning's miracle than, say, the occupants of most tour buses pulling up along the south rim of the Grand Canyon. The point may simply be that, in Japan, as in America, Edward Abbey's "industrial tourism" exerts its deadening effect.

The pace of our contemporary culture—the speed of our transportation and our mass media alike—makes it harder to find the meditative openness for which Ryōanji was designed. It seems pretty clear, too, that these Japanese teenagers frequently would rather eat a *hambaaga* from the golden arches of *Makudonarudo* than the cool, fresh offerings of sea and garden. They are also less likely to spend as much time as their parents did learning to write in calligraphic style. Pocket computers will remind them of characters they would otherwise have to learn through practice with a brush. The Japanese tradition of sensitivity to nature is today beset, just as American culture is, by heedless consumerism.

Japanese responsiveness to nature will certainly live on. Regardless of the changing outward face of the island, people will remember to begin their letters with a reference to the season and will continue to notice when the plum tree comes into flower, when the cherry blooms. And when the cherry branches are white, they will still gather as families beneath them, raising glasses of sake to the return of spring. Though these traditions help to alleviate the dreariness of technological life, however, they are finally no antidote to the environmental damage suffered by either Japan or America. I traveled to Japan looking for an alternative to the split between nature and culture troubling America. What I experienced was a society that, no matter how different the traditional way of life from ours, faces the same essential problems.

In his book, Ashihara compares the refreshing balance of the garden at Ryōanji to the garish advertising displays that dominate downtown buildings in Tokyo and Osaka. "How is it," he asks, "that Japanese, so attentive to the design of exquisitely beautiful interior spaces, end up with such unsightly building exteriors? The only explanations I can find are in the priority given interior over exterior space that arises from the attitude toward garden scenery viewed from within and the characteristics of the 'architecture oriented to the floor.'" Looking at his photographs of building exteriors in Tokyo's Shibuya quarter, I can see what he means. Arrows, flashing neon signs, and towers erected on top of the buildings just to hold more ads combine to shatter any sense of architectural integrity. But looking at them quickly, before I focus on the *kanji* within the advertisements, I see nothing foreign to the disorder of Times Square or Los Angeles.

This visual connection strengthens my growing impression that, while the Japanese genius for nature has been expressed microcosmically and our American contribution has been in the development of national parks and wilderness areas, we both suffer from a tendency to celebrate the precious aspects of nature hermetically. Just as Ryōanji is enclosed within a wall, so too our wilderness areas are bounded by a congressional mandate, decreeing that within them there shall be no permanent building, lumbering, or motorized vehicles. The Wilderness Act of 1964 erected a high wall to protect and define a series of precious landscapes. The negative implication of such a distinction, though, is that outside the wall nature can be exploited without restraint, that cities are "beyond the pale," outside the sheltering wall of wilderness. New York, like Tokyo, shows the danger of such distinctions.

Perhaps our two very different experiences of space have brought Japanese and Americans to the same predicament. Japan has been a densely populated country for centuries, with a great deal of its terrain too mountainous to support much settlement. The southern plain has thus been dominated by an urban corridor since the seventeenth century, when it included the world's two largest cities. Small wonder that the Japanese genius so early developed an inward appreciation for nature, or that emblematic celebrations of the seasons such as *bonsai* and *hanami*, or "flower-viewing," should remain essen-

tial even as the Japanese strive to sustain economic
growth on their crowded islands. America, well into
the present century, felt empty to the settlers from
Europe. In the rush to have some visible impact on
the land, we achieved a record of natural despoliation
distressing even to ourselves. By the outbreak of the
Civil War, vast herds of buffalo had been slaugh-
tered, and much of New England had been defor-
ested. Our wilderness areas were a belated decision
to draw the line, remanding a few last patches of
unspoiled nature into protective custody.

I celebrate the genius of protective and enhancing
enclosure that has brought us the gardens of Japan
and the wilderness legislation of America. But their
hermetic limitations become clearer as we confront
the global nature of environmental devastation in
our time. Neither the garden at Ryōanji nor Alaska's
Gates of the Arctic can be separated from the larger
degradation of life on earth. Natural integrity can
never be exclusive. Following my visit to Matsushima, hundreds of square miles of Prince William
Sound were covered with oil slick, as blackened seals,
otters, fish, and birds washed ashore. The millions
of acres of wilderness set aside in the interior of that
state can never correct or compensate for such a dis-
aster in the area traded off to industrial and commercial development. Nor can the *bonsai* of Hiroshima replace or make up for the disappearing rain
forests of Brazil. Carefulness identifies the mountains with the sea, and sees the balance rooted in the
woods of opposing hemispheres. The love of nature
must be comprehensive.

The environmental disasters suffered by, and perpetrated by, Japan and America do not mean that our natural visions of nature were false, nor that the hermetic beauties of garden and wilderness were a mistake. They show instead that these insights must now be developed further. In a game of Go, the enclosing energies of black and white propel the game beyond boxes and into a swirl of interfolding patterns—a beautiful complexity of design beyond either player's intention or control. In his essay "The Land Ethic," from *A Sand County Almanac* (1949), Aldo Leopold describes human history as an extension of ethical relations to broader and broader circles of life, and finally to the land itself. For Leopold, such a mature ethical vision will grow out of "love, respect, and admiration for land, and a high regard for its value. By value, I of course mean something far broader than mere economic value; I mean value in the philosophical sense." Love for the land has been nurtured in the garden, heightened in the wilderness. Now, perhaps, we can find the ways to express and enact it more expansively, more consistently.

Literature, in conveying the Japanese tradition of sensitivity to nature, did not mislead me. Poets of nature are not policy-makers but prophets, telling us what we need to do if we are to remember where we are. In America, as in Japan, we have our prophets. Thoreau, one of the first writers to point America to the East, serves as a bridge between America and Ja-

pan today, in his statement: "In wildness is the preservation of the world." John Muir, as much as he
admired Thoreau, objected that Concord was no
place to experience nature. What could that region
of towns and farms, puckerbrush and second-growth
woods, have to do with wildness? When Muir came
up with his own version of Thoreau's credo, he said,
"In God's wilderness is the preservation of the
world." For him, the sacred expression of wildness
demanded the vastness and the dramatic contrasts
provided by the western wilderness. What Thoreau,
and the Japanese, may have understood, however, is
that wildness is finally a quality of experience as
much as an outward fact. A suburban creek, or the
electrically dimmed sky above a city, can still be wild
to one who brings to it openness of eye and spirit.
A pattern of rocks and gravel can refresh and inspire
city dwellers just as a passage through the high
peaks can.

Wildness is thus an inward and essential state
about which the wildness, like the garden, can remind us. In order to encourage such wild awareness,
Thoreau urges that, wherever we may find ourselves, we "live in infinite expectation of the dawn."
In much the same way, Bashō strengthens our natural identity with his simple, integral picture of life
within the flowering world:

> *Asagao ni*
> *ware wa meshi kuu*
> *otoko kana*

I am one
who eats his breakfast
gazing at the morning-glories.
(trans. R. H. BLYTH)

Recalling our own naturalist legacies, and learning about each other's, perhaps Japanese and Americans can learn how to value nature on both sides of the wall. No part of the earth is less precious, natural, or "wild" because it lies outside congressionally drawn and protected bounds. In the same way, the Ryōanji sea depends upon the beauty of the Inland Sea: they ratify one another. The placement of each stone in the gravel reflects the larger, nonhierarchical balance of nature.

We look at *bonsai* to remember the pine islands of a bay that has been cultivated by the wind. We hike into the wilderness not just to climb the mountains, but also to see grasses shining with dew. Looking outward, looking inward, we regain our bearings as human beings in community, sustained by and celebrating the physical earth.

CAT'S CRADLE

EVEN AFTER ALL THOSE HAIKU BEGINNING WITH *haru*—the season's name—Japanese spring still astonished me. Spring is a nonseason in Vermont. Our summer's dominant chord is *green*—thick stands of dusty grass beside corn fields, the shine of lawns mown twice a week, and century maples darkening toward August after absorbing all the sun that they can hold. Fall's prism splits the constituent colors out again. Asters, goldenrod, and marsh marigolds occupy the meadows, while maples give their reds back to the declining sun. Winter lasts almost half the year, yet never gets boring. When the heavy snows don't come, that means we're settling into a spell of the menacing cold that always seems to be muttering "Watch it!" But after all this pageantry, spring, coming and going at the end of April, rarely amounts to much. It's more commonly known as "mud-season," just a couple of weeks' thawing, messy transition from winter to summer. I knew that spring in Kyoto, by contrast, would be lovely, and imagined cherry trees scattered with white blossoms, resembling the apple trees that flowered briefly in our backyard at home.

My first surprise, with a mind intent on cherries' whiteness, was the explosion of *plum* trees in our Kyoto neighborhood. Plums are everywhere along the cobbled streets that wind near Kiyomizu Temple. And since they bloom several full weeks ahead of the cherries, there are few other signs of spring competing for the eye. Reading back through Bashō I discovered that, though I had never quite registered it before, he often calls attention to the plum's *introduction* of the season. For him, too, that profusion of flowers saturated with purple and pink was always a jolt. In one haiku, he writes,

> *Suddenly the sun rose*
> *To the scent of plum-blossoms*
> *Along the mountain path.*

R. H. Blyth (whose translation this is) calls attention to the Japanese word *notto* beginning the second line. He says its function is rhythmic, conveying the season's "jerk to the mind of the poet." And not just to the mind of the poet, I can testify. Flowering when the air is still cold and the sky and ground gray, the plum announced the earth's awakening in the most emotional of colors.

Just as the unfolding petals registered the rising temperatures, their deepening color caused human residents of Kyoto, too, to open up. As we walked the sidewalks, shoulders still hunched against the cold, the plum trees straightened us up and made us feel our own pulse in the season's. The plum blossoms, in their earliness and isolation from other vernal effects, almost seemed an overture, a raising of the curtain. So Bashō implies in another of his haiku:

> *The spring scene*
> *Is well-nigh prepared:*
> *The moon and plum-blossoms.*
>
> (trans. R. H. BLYTH)

This poem and the Kyoto spring each helped me feel the meaning of the other: celebration and expectation met in one moment, expressing the imminent communion of spring.

The next surprise, just when I felt that the cherries could never match the impact of plums in the wintry air, was the *profusion* of cherry blossoms. I was expecting neither the abundance of blossoms on each tree nor the showy double and triple varieties that were everywhere. A friend pointed to one flower so full that it resembled a rose and said that it was called a *yaezakura*, or "octuple cherry." The sky brightened from the pinkish white flooding the trees, and the crowds surging through our neighborhood seemed drunk with it all. I remember standing in Maruyama Park near a huge, ancient cherry loaded with so many blossoms that bamboo trellises and platforms were required to support them. It seemed as if an entire orchard had been gathered onto a single trunk. A crowd of people stood around the tree, mothers murmuring to children, lovers holding hands—everyone just grinning up at those extravagantly blossoming boughs above our heads.

With spring, pilgrims began to appear on the Kiyomizumichi, the main road that climbed up into our neighborhood. These were often people who had recently retired and were fulfilling a lifelong vow to travel to the ancient temple on foot and stand beneath its waterfalls. Dressed in white and wearing the pilgrim's broad straw hat, they walked along jingling the bells attached to their bamboo staffs. We too were planning a spring jaunt, during the period known as "Golden Week" in Japan when, what with a break in the school calendar and the lovely weather, half the country goes on holiday at once. Having gulped and bought a one-week Japan Rail Pass for five, studied the map of Japan spread out on our dining room table, and made reservations for each leg of our journey on the Shinkansen we felt ready to brave this rolling party.

We started off by traveling east to Tokyo across Japan's central island of Honshū. For several festive days we visited friends, attended some Noh plays, took a tourist cruise down the Sumidagawa, and made a jaunt to the nearby Tokugawa shrine, set among the mountains, waterfalls, and cryptomeria trees of Nikkō. In Tokyo, too, the weather and cherry blossoms were absolutely at their prime. But over these diverting days lay the shadow of our next stop: next, we were going to be taking the Shinkan-sen all the way back across Honshū for a visit to Hiroshima. After our idyllic time in Japan, it felt as if we were coming to an unavoidable settling up with history.

Rita and I had decided it was important for our children to see this site where an atom bomb destroyed a city. Registering what had really happened there seemed essential for responsible citizens of their generation. But our agreement on this point was a nervous one. I had been to Hiroshima's Peace Park and Museum on my previous trip to Japan and knew how shattering the exhibits there were. Displays showed how the central city turned, instantly, to dust, and how people miles away from the blast had shards of glass driven through their bodies.

Actually, Rachel, Matthew, and Caleb had all decided they wanted to go to Hiroshima, anyway. Our friend Sam Nagara, whom we visited in Tokyo and who had stayed with us in Kyoto, is a survivor of the blast. At the time of the explosion, he was attending a junior high school at the outskirts of Hiroshima and was far enough away to escape burning or maiming. But since turning fifty he has experienced increasing problems with radiation sickness. Our kids were captivated by Sam's high-spirited, independent approach to life and impressed by what he had said to them about the necessity to prevent another nuclear war and, in other ways as well, to protect the natural environment.

The children had also been busily folding paper cranes for the statue in Hiroshima's Peace Park.

They had read a book called *Sadako and the Thousand Cranes* about a girl of Sam's generation who was in Hiroshima when the bomb dropped and who eventually died of the radiation's effects. While hospitalized for the final time, she began the project of folding a thousand paper cranes, motivated by a traditional Japanese belief that anyone who did so would be cured of illness. Although she died with the thousand still not finished, her classmates made the rest of them for her. Since then children from around the world have folded countless cranes in her memory and have dedicated them to world peace. Rachel, Matthew, and Caleb brought strings of them to add to the garlands already blanketing the slim bronze statue of Sadako reaching upward to a flying crane.

Another factor in the dread I felt as this trip to Hiroshima approached was that we would be touring the museum's painful exhibit with a Japanese family. Our Kyoto friend Hitomi had insisted that we let her sister and nieces, who lived in that city, act as our guides. We arrived in Hiroshima to find that her sister Furumi was much like Hitomi, petite, alert, and enjoying this chance to use her excellent English. The two daughters were eight and eleven, tall, slim girls, with matching bangs and glasses. Hiromi, the elder, delighted in trying out her own English phrases (learned from television). The morning was fine, and there was a brisk breeze from the ocean. With its broad avenues and large, beautifully landscaped parks, Hiroshima is one of the most attractive cities in Japan. One is reminded by its very spaciousness, though, that the flowered avenues radiate from the cataclysm of ground-zero. We began by spending an hour walking around the Peace Park together, admiring the flowers and hanging our paper cranes on Sadako's statue. We were circling around the visit to the museum itself, putting it off as long as possible.

I was anxious about the prospect of having to talk and be an appreciative guest while gazing at pictures of what the bomb had done to the people of Hiroshima. As it happened, though, I was saved from that trial by the isolating effects of technology. Everyone was handed a headset with a taped audio-tour to the exhibit, in Japanese or English. Duly plugged in, we walked past the glass cases in a straggling line of adults and children, not needing to find words of reaction but also forced to pause longer than we would have wished before certain nearly unbearable images. The tour took about an hour. When it was finished we handed our headsets in and walked outdoors to gather in a wordless knot on one of the walks of the Peace Park.

This was the moment when something astonishing happened. I don't know whether Furumi had planned for it or if she was simply improvising in an inspired way. She rummaged through her purse and came out with little pieces of string, knotted into circles, handing one to her girls and one to Rachel, who looked at it in astonishment until she saw that the sisters were beginning to play cat's cradle with theirs. Before long they were in a three-way game, with elaborate patterns of finger-stretched string being carefully slipped from hand to hand. Then the boys, who'd never played before, got in on the action. Furumi had plenty of string to go around, and the kids' intentness upon their game gave us all something to look at and laugh about, standing in the Hiroshima sunshine. We remained there for a long time, the children trading Japanese and American variants of cat's cradle and inventing new forms in which five or six little hands were sometimes working together at once to pluck new rays from those novas of string.

Before we caught our train back to Kyoto, we went with our hosts for an *hanami* picnic in a downtown park. Furumi spread out a cloth for us on the grass amid many other parties of Japanese, older men and women dressed in their nicest clothes, young couples in short sleeves. People were enjoying the special confections of the season and drinking from flasks of sake or thermoses of spring tea. Near us on a large island of mats was a club of jolly retirees, singing under the leadership of two kimono-clad hostesses hired for the occasion.

The trees were still white with blossoms, but it was the stage of the cherry season when the petals had begun to drift down almost continuously. They covered the park's large pond, where carp nosed at each new oval of white settling noiselessly on the water's surface. Rachel scooped up double handfuls from the drifts of fallen flowers on the gravel walk, then let them stream away from her in the wind. She seemed the embodiment of the *kanji* for the *sakura*, or "cherry"—a picture of a tree with a little woman beside it. Flower-viewing on such a day, we felt as if we were in an April snow flurry in Vermont. The exhilarating silliness of it all called to mind this haiku of Bashō's:

> *Under the cherry-trees,*
> *On soup, and fish-salad and all,*
> *Flower petals.*
>
> (trans. R. H. BLYTH)

If I had read this poem before going to Japan, I would probably have connected it with the writer's characteristic emphasis on life's transience. Here in the Japanese spring, though, I could hear him laughing, too, as the flowers just kept floating down.

Sharing the spring with this Japanese family, with cherry petals behind our ears and between our shoelaces, was the best start to sharing history, and even the history of our own century. Sitting in the snow of cherry petals together, it was also easier to understand Thoreau's phrase "the friendship of the seasons" and to hear the depth of Bashō's declaration in *Oku no Hosomichi* that "life itself is a journey." So easily we give our hearts to suffering old wars and imagining new ones, and our minds to poring over bank statements. But walking out under the flower-bright sky, we can also remember larger forces at work in the world.

Because we had planned a visit to the famous castle at Himeji after saying goodbye to Furumi and her daughters, we didn't get back to Kyoto until almost ten o'clock that night. And for some reason, at the end of that long, draining day, there was an unusually slow line at the taxi stand outside the train station. As our weary family stood waiting for a cab that would take us back to baths and futons at our Kiyomizu apartment, Matthew pulled from his pocket a loop of string that the girls had presented him at the conclusion of their game together. He stretched it on his hands and tried to remember how to begin pulling it into a pattern with his fingers. When he was just beginning to get frustrated, he was startled to feel a tap on his shoulder from behind. It was a silver-haired Japanese businessman standing in the taxi line. Without addressing a word to Matthew, he held up one finger solemnly, then reached in with the forefingers and thumbs of both hands to show how the next phase of cat's cradle worked. Matthew's enough of a little Vermonter to feel comfortable with nonverbal communication, and the two of them worked together silently and intently for the ten minutes until it was finally our turn for a taxi. While either Matthew or his dignified friend held the outlines taut, the other would squeeze the edges in toward the center, then open those new points out, passing from hand to hand the ever more beautifully articulated boundary of string.